The Organic Entrepreneur Economy

The Entrepreneur and Community Infrastructures that Fix and Grow Economies...Immediately

Seth Meinzen + Steve Meinzen

Contributing Authors:

Barry J Crocker, Mark W. Dickey,
Christopher Doroh, Dr. Bernard Franklin,
Lisa Franklin, Jo Anne Gabbert, Matthew Hart,
Jeff Kaczmarek, Danny Lobina,
Corey J. Mehaffy, Michie P. Slaughter,
Brien M. Starner

Contents

Authors

Contributing Authors

Acknowledgements

All of the Authors would like to thank the many supporters and partners who worked tirelessly to make this book possible. As well as the countless entrepreneurs and organizations that aided our efforts as we developed and implemented the many processes discussed in The Organic Entrepreneur Economy.

A short-list of people and organizations that went above and beyond are:

> **Doug Dick** – Editor
> **Faith Meinzen** – Editor
> **Matt Huebschmann** – Artist
> **Beth Flemington** – Designer and Publisher
> **White Rim Books** - Publisher

Specific Acknowledgements from our Authors are:

Danny Lobina - I would like to thank Moberly Area Community College, Moberly Area Chamber of Commerce, and Moberly Area Economic Development Corp for partnering with the SBTDC on the Grow Mid-Missouri project. Also the SBA and SBTDC for providing great programs for entrepreneurs and small businesses. I would also thank my friends and family for being supportive of my work. Without their support I could not do what I do successfully.

Barry J. Crocker - I would like to thank my wife Laurie, and my kids Ezra & Mitch. Their love and support is unwavering and that is what drives me to be the best I can be. Also my parents Dave & Debbie who instilled an entrepreneurial spirit in me at a young age when they started their own successful brick & mortar business. Finally, thanks to my partners Seth, Claire, Chris, Steve & their families. Without everyone listed above, none of this would have been possible.

Corey J. Mehaffy - I would like to express my gratitude to the Boards of Directors and staffs of Moberly Area Economic Development Corporation, Moberly Area Community College and Moberly Area Chamber of Commerce for their vision and collaboration to create the Grow Mid-Missouri Organic Environment in support of our local entrepreneurs. I am particularly grateful for the numerous business and civic leaders who volunteer their time and expertise in support of this program. Special thanks should be given to our entrepreneurs' for their commitment to bring these ideas to reality and make these important investments in our communities. I am forever indebted to my family and friends for their continued encouragement of my work.

Christopher Doroh - I want to thank God for this opportunity, my wife Katie for supporting me from the beginning, and my mother for always believing in me. Last but not least I want to thank my former professor Ron Harvey who emulates the entrepreneurial spirit and introduced me to the world of entrepreneurship.

Brien M. Starner - I would like to thank the Blue Springs EDC and both members and participants of Grow Blue Springs to support our local efforts.

Mark W. Dickey - The Lee's Summit Chamber of Commerce is extremely grateful to the strong partnership with KCP&L, Jackson County, ED Department and AdventureTech. Their investment in Boost Lee's Summit's launch and ongoing operations has assured a new generation of businesses will jettison from ideas to the marketplace. We also thank our network of coordinators, mentors, business resources, coaches and event sponsors for their dedication and determination in making Lee's Summit the place to start and succeed in business.

Steve Meinzen - This book was a rare opportunity to work with a gifted son with his supportive wife as well as collaborate with a rare and beautiful woman whom I was blessed to meet 39 years ago, my wife Faith.

Dr. Bernard Franklin - I want to thank the Kauffman Foundation and MCC Penn Valley for providing me the opportunity gain the insights on entrepreneurship necessary to create this collaborative process and to make communities more sustainable. Additionally I want to thank my family and friends for all of the support they have provided to make this possible!

Lisa Franklin - Thanks for my many friends and colleagues throughout the Economic Development profession who have supported me throughout my career. Additionally I want to thank my family, kids, and husband for the support they have given me to achieve this next milestone!

Seth Meinzen – I am incredibly grateful to the many entrepreneurs, mentors, and advisors that have worked with me as an entrepreneur over the last 9 years. Everyone's support and advice has helped me become and achieve what I have. Specifically I would like to thank all of my co-authors in this book, as this collaborative experience has truly culminated in a great result. Finally I would like to thank my parents, my loving wife Claire, and new daughter Norah for their support. Last and most importantly I want to thank my Lord and Savior Jesus Christ for providing me this opportunity.

The Organic Entrepreneur Economy

The Entrepreneur and Community Infrastructures that Fix and Grow Economies...Immediately

Preface:

Entrepreneurial State of the Authors

The book *The Organic Entrepreneur Economy* started as a passionate debate between several Kansas City-native entrepreneurs and myself on whether entrepreneurship could be streamlined. We wondered why starting and growing a business was so complex, and if it could be simplified. Our hypothesis was that entrepreneurs lacked a GPS-guide of sorts to lead them through the startup and growth process and connect them to support programs like mentors, resources, and investors along the way. We speculated that if this GPS-guide was placed in the hands of the community, entrepreneurs, and government and civic leaders that entire economies could be quickly stabilized and grown. Little did any of us know that a mere 7-years later, the hypothetical entrepreneur GPS-guide would be built in Kansas City in a manner that exponentially grew the technology and startup community.

During the creation of the Organic Environment methodology that led to authoring of *The Organic Entrepreneur Economy*, Kansas City's successful and notable entrepreneurs regularly asked how the community could be engaged as they strongly believed the masses defined the culture, which in turn was the economic engine that empowered entrepreneurship. Interestingly one entrepreneur used this analogy to describe the importance of a community and its culture: a parent's perspective of the benefit and security of the entrepreneurial profession will decide whether they encourage their kids to start a new business or work for a corporation. Additionally a community's culture will help guide aspiring entrepreneurs' decisions to either take the leap to start a business or play it safe with a job. These realizations provided an understanding for the importance of a community, its culture, and the power of communication within a city or region.

Upon realizing the importance of the community and fostering a supportive culture, we decided that it was more important to promote those facets to the Kansas City community and beyond than to promote the individual accomplishments of the team or Advisory Experts...until now! Thus it is likely you may have never heard about the organizations or initiatives discussed in *The Organic Entrepreneur Economy* (i.e. StartKC, StartPath, EvisThrive, and Evis Consulting) because fostering increased community confidence in entrepreneurship and evolving a supportive culture in Kansas City necessitated that these entities remain in the background and out of the limelight to foster organic growth.

The unique strength of *The Organic Entrepreneur Economy* and the Organic Environment methodology is the connection it makes between entrepreneurs and communities. This is less an implementation guide and more of an organic methodology to understand the mindsets of entrepreneurs and a community before outlining the steps needed to orchestrate sustainable economic growth. *(Though a program and implementation guide for The Organic Entrepreneur Economy does exist and is available through Evis Consulting, it is not described in detail within this book.)* This methodology was realized organically through years of entrepreneurial experiences in starting, growing, and supporting businesses and orchestrating Kansas City community support for entrepreneurship. From this experience, a working model was developed to achieve exponential entrepreneur and community economic growth and success.

For those of us who authored *The Organic Entrepreneur Economy* and built the Organic Environment methodology, the goal was to increase the community and entrepreneurial successes in Kansas City, and understand how to repeat these results systematically. After years of focused efforts, success in Kansas City finally became apparent. In 2010, to determine if success could be replicated, the Organic Environment methodology was contracted by the Economic Development Corporations and/or Chambers of Commerce in three additional small to medium-sized cities: Blue Springs, Lees Summit, and Moberly, Missouri. Each build delivered strong city or region-wide successes in terms of a supportive community and culture, as well as fostering significant entrepreneurial growth. This was an incredible milestone, as it was my perception that most entrepreneurial ecosystems were built within a specific city's or region's community or entrepreneurial base and struggled to be applicable or successful in other cities or regions. Additionally each city reported noticeable changes in their community and entrepreneurs in as little as 6 months and achieved their definition of success in a cool 18 - 24 months. This is significant, as many entrepreneur strategies we researched seemed to take at least 20 to 30 years to reach economic success. These milestones were significant, as it means the methodology is organically applicable to the community and entrepreneurs in any city or region, and thereby could aid any government and its civic leaders in stabilizing and growing their economies!

The Organic Entrepreneur Economy book rarely references university, institutional, or industry-specific research, other than that from the Kauffman Foundation. This is not because it isn't important or doesn't matter - this couldn't be farther from the truth. Rather, the Organic Environment methodology was developed in the "market" and proven to work in multiple cities, as well as urban and rural regions. In this time of great economic uncertainty, it was decided to publish the book in its "street-smart" format and then follow up with research and references in an updated version later on.

I engaged the advisors and experts that have helped us design and implement this Organic Environment methodology to contribute to the authorship of *The Organic Entrepreneur Economy*. These Advisory Experts *(referenced as Contributing Authors on the cover)* were previously known for their contributions to entrepreneurship, community development, and economic development in the United States and around the world. This provides an enhanced level of credibility, as these Advisory Experts only agreed to support *The Organic Entrepreneur Economy* after they became convinced of its methodological and economical validity in cities and regions.

The Advisory Experts, their experiences, and a brief summary of their contributions are as follows:

Michie P. Slaughter – Founding President of the Kauffman Foundation's Center for Entrepreneurial Leadership and Former Vice President of Human Resources of Marion Labs. Michie's contributions pertained to insights for how to setup and operate entrepreneur programs, as well as insights for how to ensure each program was scalable. *(bio in back of book)*

Dr. Bernard Franklin – Formerly the President of the MCC Penn Valley Community College, Formerly the Executive Director of Kauffman Scholars within the Kauffman Foundation, and Currently the President of Junior Achievement of Middle America. Bernard's contributions pertained to insights on how best to educate the community and entrepreneurs. *(bio in back of book)*

Jo Anne Gabbert – Serial Entrepreneur, Angel Investor, former President of Bicknell Family Holding Company, former Project Lead of the Kansas City Chamber of Commerce's Big 5 Entrepreneur Initiative, founder and former Chief Executive Officer of Adams-Gabbert & Associates management consulting firm and current owner and CEO of JAG Portfolio Services. Jo Anne's contributions pertained to insights for how to best engage entrepreneurs, support programs, and investors, as well as perspective for how to train government and civic leaders to implement the entrepreneur and community programs *(called Infrastructures). (bio in back of book)*

Jeff Kaczmarek – Formerly the President of Kansas City, Missouri's Economic Development Corporation, and currently the Executive Director, Department of Economic Development - Prince William County, Virginia *(a suburb of Washington D.C.).* Jeff's contributions pertained to initially introducing the Organic Environment's methodology and infrastructures in Kansas City *(within StartKC)* and collaborations on how to achieve the best outcomes. *(bio in back of book)*

Lisa Franklin - Manager, Economic Development and LocationOne at Kansas City Power & Light. Lisa's contributions pertained to how to gain support from government and civic leaders, as well as insights for how to achieve individual and mass support for the methodologies and infrastructures. *(bio in back of book)*

Brien M. Starner – President of Blue Springs, Missouri Economic Development Corporation and Facilitator of GrowBlueSprings.com *(which utilizes the Organic Environment's methodology).* Brien's contributions pertained to being the first replicating city, offering insights for how to cater the infrastructures to each city or region, and how to scale the methodology for systematic implementation. *(bio in back of book)*

Danny Lobina - Director of the Small Business Technology Development Center (a program of the U.S. Small Business Administration) at Moberly-area Community College, Small Business Advisor, and Co-founder of GrowMidMo.com *(which utilizes the Organic Environment's methodology).* Danny's contributions pertained to insights for how the methodology and infrastructures could work seamlessly with the Small Business Administration's Small Business Development Centers spread throughout the United States, within universities, and with other higher education institutions, as well as insights into how to coach entrepreneurs based on their true needs. *(bio in back of book)*

Mark W. Dickey – Vice President of Lee's Summit, Missouri's Chamber of Commerce, and Administrator for BoostLeesSummit.com *(which utilizes the Organic Environment's methodol-*

ogy). Mark's contributions pertained to being the first Chamber of Commerce to facilitate the adoption of the methodology and critical insights for how to better utilize the community to generate support and entrepreneurial growth. *(bio in back of book)*

Matthew Hart - Author of *Middlework: Unlock the Underestimated and Unappreciated Secret to Success*, and Vice President at Arise Virtual Solutions. Matt's contributions pertained to insights for how to gain involvement throughout the community and insights for how to mobilize the mass followers in the community. *(bio in back of book)*

Corey J Mehaffy – President, Moberly Area Economic Development Corporation, Co-founder/Facilitator of GrowMidMo. com *(which utilizes the Organic Environment's methodology)*, and founder of the economic development consulting firm C J Mehaffy, LLC. Corey's contributions pertained to insights for how to utilize the Organic Environment methodology to establish the entrepreneurship and community support in rural areas and across multiple counties, as well as insights for how to use standard economic development tools to multiply the effects of entrepreneurship for a city or region. *(bio in back of book)*

The social entrepreneurs from Evis Consulting who designed the Organic Environment methodology behind *The Organic Entrepreneur Economy* are:

Seth Meinzen *(Narrator and co-Author)* - Social Entrepreneur *(focused on starting businesses that help others in the community)*, Co-founder of nine Entrepreneurial Businesses, Recognized Community and Culture Builder, as well as an Advocate for

Entrepreneurship. Seth's contributions, in true entrepreneurial fashion, span every aspect of *The Organic Entrepreneur Economy* and have influenced every infrastructure, methodology, and guidepost. Seth's influence is not merely based in leadership, but also in his fearless drive to figure out what worked and what didn't with entrepreneurs and the community. *(bio in back of book)*

Steve Meinzen *(co-Author)* – Executive Partner, Serial Entrepreneur, and Engineer and Marketing Manager at the John Deere Corporation. Steve's contributions are embodied in strategy and leadership and have supported *The Organic Entrepreneur Economy* from its conception. *(bio in back of book)*

Barry J Crocker – Technology and Social Media Partner, Serial Entrepreneur, and former Founder & CEO of KidsTube. com. Barry's contributions include insights on how to promote entrepreneurship and the community, as well as how to influence culture. *(bio in back of book)*

Christopher Doroh – Financial & Operating Partner and Entrepreneur. Chris's contributions are focused around connectivity to investors and the processes needed to support entrepreneurs. *(bio in back of book)*

It is important to point out that throughout this book, I - Seth Meinzen - am narrating and at times the perspective switches to we, being the Advisory Experts and Evis Consulting team. This is necessary because *The Organic Entrepreneur Economy* is a work of collaboration and needed to be written as such.

In addition to those listed as we, there have been literally hundreds if not thousands of mentors, organizations, corporations, and entrepreneurs in Kansas City and beyond that have helped shape and guide the development of this Organic Environment methodology. We are deeply grateful to all that have shared insights and provided support to bring *The Organic Entrepreneur Economy* and its Organic Environment methodology to fruition! Those involvements have resulted in the creation of over 30 entrepreneurial events, over a hundred entrepreneurial collaboration sessions, and the guidance for multitudes of entrepreneurs who have since achieved success.

I find it important to acknowledge that entrepreneurship and community development in Kansas City and elsewhere is in a constant state of evolution. Entrepreneurs, community leaders, and government and civic leaders are constantly attempting to grow their economies. In the 1990's, Ewing Marion Kauffman founded his foundation and The Center for Entrepreneurial Leadership to make significant entrepreneur impacts in Kansas City and around the world. Ironically, at the time of our passionate debate and throughout the organic build of the Organic Environment methodology, we were completely unaware of those entrepreneurs and progresses that had come before. Though it is not always possible, I am compelled to suggest that involving as many former entrepreneurial and community influencers, as well as current entrepreneur and community influencers, will only increase the results. While we proceeded with a blind eye, we now recognize the immense efforts of many who came before in Kansas City and are grateful to have been able to utilize those inroads to build the Organic Environment methodology described within *The Organic Entrepreneur Economy*. We suggest that cities and regions embrace their entrepreneurial past, as these people and organizations often carry significant influence and resources that can help entrepreneurship and the community thrive once again!

For us, helping entrepreneurs and communities achieve their dream and desired success is what is most important! We are serial entrepreneurs and community advocates who are passionate about helping others achieve success. As much as *The Organic Entrepreneur Economy* can be a game-changer for communities, entrepreneurs, governments and civic organizations in cities and regions, and most importantly their economies...it is also a passion that we all hold near and dear. So we are thrilled and humbled that God has graciously given us this opportunity to support government and civic leaders as they achieve entrepreneurial and community growth, and look forward to the opportunity of supporting many, many more.

Finally, the purpose of writing *The Organic Entrepreneur Economy* is to provide government and civic leaders and others with the "AH-HA" experience for how a community growing in tandem with entrepreneurs can be organized to create exponential success in a short period of time. To make *The Organic Entrepreneur Economy* more interesting and applicable, we paired it with stories from entrepreneurial Kansas City and insights from the Advisory Experts. This should reveal that exponential economic success is best achieved by the community and entrepreneurs when they are supported by government and civic leaders. We hope you will enjoy this ride as much as we have!

Chapter 1:

The Answer - The Organic Environment

The answer to having a growing, sustainable economy has to be entrepreneurship WITH a supportive community. Entrepreneurs are the people who start or grow businesses, which accounts for 99.7% of the U.S. employer firms. As of 2010 there were 27,900,000 small businesses in the U.S. alone. Thus entrepreneurship is the answer to creating new jobs, creating new business, and growing the economy. Entrepreneurship alone cannot grow an economy, however. Each individual entrepreneur is focused on starting or growing their specific business and an economy is sustained and grown by the environment that attracts and supports the collective businesses to start and grow together in a city or region. The reason why the great entrepreneur cities and regions, like Silicon Valley, Boston, Boulder, and now Kansas City, are able to achieve growing economies is that each has an intensely supportive community. In fact, the point when each community's support of entrepreneurs becomes the social norm, or the culture, is the moment when entrepreneurship and the economy really begin to grow toward sustainability. *The Organic Entrepreneur Economy* offers leaders the proven methodology, known as the **Organic**

Environment, that will foster entrepreneurship and develop a supportive community to produce sustainable economic growth. The most effective, efficient, and sustainable approach to implementing this Organic Environment methodology is facilitation from government and civic leaders and execution by those in the community.

> *"Economic Development has changed. The search for jobs is no longer outside the community, but rather inside. The Organic Environment's approach utilizes a proven structure to motivate the community to grow their own entrepreneurs, and thereby their economy. This is truly a step forward."*
>
> *~ Lisa Franklin*

Leaders who utilize the Organic Environment methodology will gain the understanding for why entrepreneurs start and grow businesses and what compels a community to embrace business entrepreneurship. These are the obstacles that keep most cities or regions from fostering entrepreneurial hubs and achieving a sustainable, growing economy, for the culture that fosters entrepreneurship and develops a supportive community is a natural process that takes at least 20-30 years to evolve. Without first understanding entrepreneurs AND the community, investments in business initiatives or entrepreneurial programs will likely fail in the long-run. Skipping this formative first step in the near term will result in the deceleration of creating a vibrant entrepreneurial community. Only when it is understood "why entrepreneurs start and grow businesses" and "why communities support entrepreneurs" will leaders know how to organically reduce that natural evolution of 20-30 years...down to a more manageable 18-24 months.

Answering the **why** questions unlocks the entrepreneur and community **mindsets** that provide critical **insights:** how to accelerate the creation and growth of businesses or how a community can organically embrace entrepreneurship in their city or region. These insights lay the groundwork for building the **operations** designed to organically engage the community to support the entrepreneurial masses in starting and growing their businesses. Knowing the mindsets and building the operations for entrepreneurs and the community will organically accelerate economic growth. This embodies the Organic Environment!

These mindsets and operational programs were identified while building Kansas City's early entrepreneur environment. This process was not done in a lab or from a theoretical standpoint, rather it was built over years by working directly with entrepreneurs and the community to establish the methodology. Then the Organic Environment methodology was applied to organically accelerate multiple cities' and region's economies by fostering entrepreneurial hubs with supportive communities. The Organic Environment methodology and the four infrastructures have not been scientifically validated by dou-

> *"The Organic Environment is the great equalizer allowing entrepreneurs and their community to do great things within their city or environment and to feel an intimate sense of connection."*
>
> *~Brien M. Starner*

ble-blind studies, but have and continue to produce results by guiding government and civic leaders on how to produce entrepreneur hubs, supportive community cultures, and economic successes in their cities or regions. Several notable institutional and entrepreneurial figure-heads, collectively referred to as the Advisory Experts, guided those government and civic leaders. These Advisory Experts have been so thoroughly convinced of the results that they have contributed to the authorship of *The Organic Entrepreneur Economy*. In fact, throughout the book, the narration switches from 1st person to 2nd person to showcase the collaboration and continual insights offered by the Advisory Experts.

The Organic Entrepreneur Economy's Organic Environment methodology and four infrastructures were designed by social entrepreneurs from Evis Consulting, and were guided by insights from the Advisory Experts who are and have been successful entrepreneurs, angel investors, business coaches, government & civic leaders, corporate & institutional leaders, and even the Founding President of the Kauffman Foundation's Center for Entrepreneurial Leadership. Together the social entrepreneurs and Advisory Experts have formulated and implemented a systematic methodology that has the potential to exponentially accelerate the creation and growth of entrepreneurial businesses, foster a supportive community and culture, and most importantly achieve a growing economy.

> *"The Organic Environment that worked in Kansas City and is being implemented in other cities or regions stands on the shoulders of many entrepreneurs and past community leaders."*
>
> ~ *Michie P. Slaughter*

To provide greater context for how the Organic Environment methodology and the four infrastructures are implemented by government and civic leaders to benefit their cities or regions, the Advisory Experts have added professional insights and perspectives as sidebar commentary throughout the book.

The fact is, building an Organic Environment in a city

or region and having lasting effects is an extremely complex and integrated process, which explains why it naturally takes decades for a growing entrepreneurial environment and economy to evolve. To simplify the explanation and integration, four infrastructures have been designed:

1. **Entrepreneur Social Infrastructure** – Understanding what causes entrepreneurs to start or grow businesses, and how to motivate these business builders.

2. **Community Social Infrastructure** – Understanding what causes a group of people, collectively referred to as a community, to support entrepreneurs, as well as what motivates the community to take action.

3. **Community Operational Infrastructure** – Leveraging the community and entrepreneur social infrastructures, these operational strategies must be implemented to grow a supportive community culture and a community-driven structure to foster growth in entrepreneurship.

4. **Entrepreneur Operational Infrastructure** – Leveraging the entrepreneur and community social infrastructures, these operational strategies accelerate the creation and growth of entrepreneurial ventures and track progress.

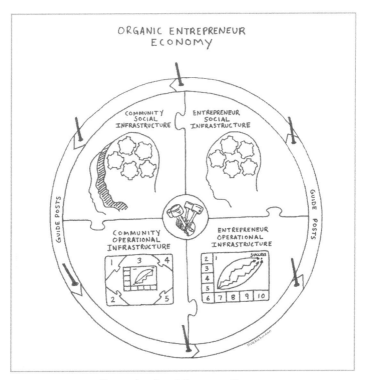

The complete *Organic Entrepreneur Economy*:
Organic Environment, four Infrastructures and 6 Guideposts

The four infrastructures embody the Organic Environment methodology to support government and civic leaders' efforts in building supportive communities to foster entrepreneurship. More importantly, though, is the fact that the infrastructures can be customized to fit any city's or region's community, desired culture, or desired entrepreneurial focus. This allows government and civic leaders to finally gain the tools and processes they need to foster entrepreneurship alongside a supportive community in their city or region.

Government and civic leaders are experts at utilizing physical infrastructures to build their cities and regions and achieve a competitive edge for attracting outside businesses in the global marketplace. However, the struggle to date has been how to utilize these infrastructures to foster a community that supports the risks and business startups that come with entrepreneurs. These infrastructures that foster a supportive community or strong entrepreneurial success have not been in existence, until now. So understandably the concept of a methodology systematically growing an economy through the managed development of a community, its culture, and its entrepreneurs no doubt seems foreign or even fictional. However, as the Advisory Experts as well as government and civic leaders will attest, the Organic Environment not only remedies this void with the Social and Operational Infrastructures, but also provides the tracking to measure the real world validity of these economic outcomes.

To achieve these economic outcomes requires an equal, organic focus on fostering support from the community and on guiding entre-

"Simply providing a sparsely used solution is no solution at all. The Infrastructures provide the critical understanding necessary to interpret the needs and motivations of the community and entrepreneurs. A purposefully growing economy, resulting from a network of programs facilitated by experts based on defined needs, is the goal. Understanding and implementing a defined system, with established metrics and reporting, and achieving proven goals is the path to economic success."

~ Jeff Kaczmarek

"In the 1800's it was all about creating physical infrastructures for growth, and now the need is for social infrastructures to strengthen and foster entrepreneurship."

~ Brien M. Starner

preneurs on how to start and grow businesses. Thus the Organic Environment methodology is embodied in *The Organic Entrepreneur Economy.*

Chapter 2:

The Entrepreneurial State

At the outset of debating how to streamline entrepreneurship in Kansas City, we faced the monumental challenge of figuring out how to formulate the process, and then even more difficult, was deciding how to describe it. At that time, entrepreneurship was considered a phenomenon that was as likely to generate jobs and a boost in the economy as it was to bankrupt the entrepreneur and those trying to support it.

In an effort to gain clarity during one of our first meetings, we had to validate the early concept with Larry Lee, who was the Director of Technology Development for the University of Missouri-Kansas City's Small Business and Technology Development Center, who agreed to meet with us for 30 minutes, but graciously gave us almost 3 hours. Mr. Lee, who has since become the Director for Northwest Missouri State University's Center for Innovation and Entrepreneurship, posed some tough

"The process to build any entrepreneur base, especially in Kansas City, relies heavily on embracing the entrepreneurs that came before. These successful entrepreneurs have immense influence in the community."

~ Michie P. Slaughter

questions: How are you able to financially help the entrepreneur masses, identify the businesses that are most likely to succeed, and provide the most amount of time and financial resources with them? He also asked what we considered an entrepreneur to be? These were tough questions that we couldn't answer at the time, but knew we would need to answer to achieve success. So we researched to find these answers, as well as a way to describe and quantify the importance of entrepreneurship in Kansas City, or any city or region.

What we found was that entrepreneurs are the backbone of the United States economy, as these small businesses are responsible for 60-80% of all job creation and half of all non-farm gross domestic product. Entrepreneurs have a unique talent to combine the motivation to harness ideas with the determination to build them into revenue-generating businesses. According to the Small Business Administration (SBA), 90% of all net new jobs come from entrepreneurial businesses less than 1-year old. So what is the value of entrepreneurship?

The value of entrepreneurship to a community may be best understood when quantified. The SBA estimates there are 500,000 new businesses created each year. The Kauffman Foundation's Index of Entrepreneurial Activity goes further to identify that for every 100,000 people, 300 people

> *"Entrepreneurship is incredibly valuable to every city or region. More importantly though, every community should determine how to focus or foster business creation and growth. Silicon Valley's economy has reached the pinnacle in the technology sector, allowing other communities to achieve pinnacle growth in other sectors. Communities throughout the world are reaching for the top with their economies. This is an exciting time!"*
>
> *~ Lisa Franklin*

will start a new business each month. This activity becomes significant in light of 1st year startup spending statistics from the likes of the Small Business Administrations and U.S. Census Bureau, which conservative average expenditures are $24,700 per year. This means a community with 100,000 people, there are 300 new businesses each spending $24,700 annually, or roughly $7,410,000, as well as generating 90% of all the net new jobs. More importantly, these new businesses are actually providing a constant flow of new customers into a city's or region's economy, and can even spur growth to existing businesses.

Thinking back to Larry Lee's question, we realized that we defined anyone who starts or grows a revenue-generating business as an entrepreneur. Though every entrepreneur will have a different type, format, and growth target that they want to achieve, we decided to streamline the path to startup and growth for all entrepreneurs. While this seemed overly optimistic at the time, this definition likely attributed to our eventual success. To test this broad definition of entrepreneurship, we had to demonstrate to ourselves and others that they all existed. It was recognized that Kansas City had pockets of entrepreneurs that were grouped together, almost like cliques in high school. The government and civic leaders, as well as the Advisory Experts on board at the time, acknowledged that entrepreneurship was the BIG opportunity for Kansas City's economy, but it first required seeking out and finding these disparate groups of entrepreneurs.

After some creative imagineering through the use of Bernard Franklin's methodology, we constructed an event called startFEST+DEMO to showcase 10 startups in front of their entrepreneurial peers. We hosted the event at the Boulevard Brewery. In case the 10 startups weren't a big enough draw, we figured free beer might be! StartFEST+DEMO attracted 150 entrepreneurs and professionals, but the qualitative results of the event, or the social metrics, were even more compelling. For during startFEST+DEMO, the participants instantly began to collaborate, share ideas and concepts, and find ways to support each other's growth. The creative energy and excitement in the room was infectious, and entrepreneurs almost instinctively begin recruiting other "non-entrepreneurs" to embrace their passion and take the leap into business ownership. This energized not only aspiring entrepreneurs, but also invigorated those who were already in the game.

Prior to this event, it was thought that this type of energy only existed in places like Boston, Boulder or the iconic Silicon Valley. Even more exciting for us was the fact that the engaging atmosphere of the startFEST+DEMO echoed throughout the city and region for a whole week, as we fielded calls and emails asking when the next event would be. However, we realized that this was a one-time event and the enthusiasm would wane over time. So we knew we had to find a way to keep the atmosphere "always on" and the momentum continually building.

Entrepreneurship has always been perceived to be more of a naturally occurring and chaotic phenomenon than one resulting from an orchestrated strategy. So how can a city or region use entrepreneurship as an answer if they cannot increase the supply or rate of progress? This question will begin to be addressed in Chapter 4, but the short answer is that entrepreneurs share a symbiotic and almost dependent relationship with the community. Entrepreneurship is most often grown through grassroots campaigns designed to make the community more open and encouraging to new and existing business ownership. This is exactly what was orchestrated in Kansas City on a small scale when launching the first startFEST+DEMO event, and ultimately what was achieved on a larger scale with the Organic Environment 7 years into the future. Just as the community reached out after the startFEST+DEMO event, when Kansas City's entrepreneurs began to attract the attention of the national press the community became involved in a flurry of activities, events, and groups that celebrated the growth of entrepreneurship. From the outside it appeared that a natural progression of entrepreneurial activity had built Kansas City, when in actuality there were community operations, called infrastructures, that helped to orchestrate much of the activity behind the scenes! These infrastructures became the answer to the "always on" atmosphere that we were seeking after the first startFEST+DEMO event, which will be discussed further throughout this book.

"It is important to foster connection between entrepreneurs and government/civic leaders within a community to grow entrepreneurship. Engagement of government/ civic leaders in a community to understand entrepreneurs helps explain what the environment is and how to best help entrepreneurs."

~ Barry J Crocker

Anyone that has ever worked with an entrepreneur knows they are a driven and seemingly unpredictable bunch. I am reminded of an SBA administrator who during a panel at an SBA Young Entrepreneur Conference asked 'how she could help' entrepreneurs. Three entrepreneurs answered as follows: 1) Keep the government off my back and let me build my business, 2) Provide me with access to government contracts, and 3) Be there when I need you, but otherwise leave me alone. I remember the SBA administrator being perplexed, as the first two responses contradicted each other, and the last one required the assistance of a mind reader. Interestingly enough, while these answers seem chaotic, when entrepreneurs are grouped by the stage of their businesses these answers begin to seem rational and predictable.

As entrepreneurs start and grow businesses their needs, wants and perspectives change accordingly. The key to making sense of this is to understand the developmental stages of a new and growing business, as well as how entrepreneurs perceive and act in each stage.

The Entrepreneurial State is naturally chaotic because entrepreneurs are constantly struggling to learn and develop their businesses while being bombarded by advice from the community, which is often conflicting. This clouds the path to success, causing the natural Entrepreneurial State to be nearly impossible to analyze, measure, or even traverse for the business owner. Bringing clarity to the Entrepreneurial State requires shifting out of the natural, chaotic environment into an organized path for success that is reinforced by the community. To achieve this shift, one must understand what the perceptions of the entrepreneurs and the community are that result in specific actions, as well as how to direct both towards positive economic outcomes.

"Entrepreneurs as a whole are private, looking for resources that fit their needs. Their learning occurs after hours, at their own pace, when they are available. It's important for a community to make sure entrepreneurs have access to these resources when they need them, not when the community believes they should."

~ Corey J. Mehaffy

Before we charge into the shift that is the Organic Environment, it is important to better understand how communities have impacted entrepreneurship and their own economies, as communities are likely the missing link to exponentially growing entrepreneurship in a city or region.

Chapter 3:

State of Entrepreneurial Communities

Just as research proved the importance of entrepreneurship to an economy, we wondered if increasing the number of successful entrepreneurs could be as simple as providing access to the right programs and connectivity to the right advisors based on the stage of business. Examining the Kansas City business environment, we realized that many entrepreneurs had naturally organized into tight pods, or groupings. One such pod was led by Cameron Colby Thomson, founder of Allied Strategy and incubator Turbine Flats, and I was lucky enough to be supported by him and his network as I started my first business. Cameron and his support network would offer to provide insights into my and other startup businesses, and his network of support resources were available for further paid services. The benefit from this pod was that I knew each resource vendor was qualified and would deliver the desired service. Like the pod I was in with Cameron, each pod was informal and came without any real form of membership. Each pod's successful entrepreneurs informally mentored or coached the less experienced entrepreneurs through starting and growing their business, and also connected them to their network of qualified resources, like lawyers, accountants, software developers, etc. Most importantly, those in the pod were incredibly supportive of their fellow entrepreneurs and were willing to do almost anything to help others achieve success.

A first-time entrepreneur, or even an experienced one, had a significantly greater chance of achieving success by being in a pod. As a pod participant, an entrepreneur had a supportive "community" who intimately understood mental and financial challenges that went along with this profession, as well as how to propose suggestions in a constructive manner. A podded entrepreneur would also gain introductions to a prized network of potential customer contacts much sooner than if they were without the pod. Interestingly these small, tightly-connected pods were littered throughout the Kansas City metro area, though they rarely connected or interacted with other pods. We realized these pods were naturally occurring microcosms for what we desired to establish in Kansas City.

> *"Small groups and teams within a community cannot be connected to each other by accident. It simply takes too long, and you end up hoping for success instead of ensuring it. There must be connective tissue put into place—sensibly, and with the greater good of the community in mind."*
>
> *~ Matthew Hart*

However, government, civic, and even community leaders seeking entrepreneurial growth historically focus their efforts on building gateways to aggregate support programs (i.e. the resources, services, investors, and other entrepreneur-focused activities). These are designed to provide entrepreneurs access to the services needed to start and grow their business. The intent is to provide the support programs that will be required to overcome the myriad of business problems faced by entrepreneurs. By connecting entrepreneurs to the support program and resource vendors within the city or region, support businesses and non-profits can also benefit from the entrepreneurial businesses. This intent is admirable but misses a critical perspective: entrepreneurs starting and growing businesses rarely are able to pinpoint their challenges or diagnose their problems. This is the reason there are so many consultants! Offering support programs is like offering an answer before entrepreneurs can formulate the question.

This reminds me of a recurring conversation I have had with Darrell Brammer, Director of the Small Business Technology Development Center at the University of Central Missouri, who has been a strong partner in developing the methodology behind *The Organic Entrepreneur Economy* and has contributed to much of the success in Kansas City. Darrell mentioned that the majority of entrepreneurs that the center's counselors have met with are: 1) focused on solving problems he/she doesn't have, or 2) simply unaware of the real problems hindering their success. Darrell explains that this happens when an entrepreneur faces a challenge that is invisible to them, and rather than addressing that challenge they opt to ignore the problem and continue progress in other areas. This is often the case when

"At the first press conference for the Kauffman Foundation, the first 3 questions asked by reporters were: How much money will the foundation invest? (3 times) The answer was NONE. So while these leaders are right to focus on support infrastructures, greater focus must be placed on first understanding the entrepreneurs and their communal environment, as the Kauffman Foundation did in the 1990's. "

~ Michie P. Slaughter

entrepreneurs write 40-page business plans for a product or service that is not ready or not in the market. To right these wrongs, the counselor must first gain the trust of an entrepreneur, which requires a significant amount of time, and then the entrepreneur must be guided to self-realize the original unanswered problem that is holding back the business. *(Simply telling the entrepreneur the answer might help in that instance, but if the entrepreneur doesn't understand how that answer was identified, he/she is likely to be stuck by the same problem again.)* Only then can counselors work with them to use resources or programs to overcome the problem. A small minority of entrepreneurs, mostly the experienced or incredibly lucky ones, are able to consistently identify their problems, formulate the question of their needs, and then seek out a support program or resource to overcome the challenge. Ironically, Darrell pointed out that this minority rarely engages with them or any support program, as they already know how to find the solution.

"Many training and support programs offer solutions to a business' problems, but neglect to show how the solutions were found. This alienates the entrepreneur from the problem solving process. Training and support programs need to help entrepreneurs self-realize solutions to learn how to solve future problems and develop strong businesses."

~ Mark W. Dickey

Darrell's experience demonstrates that entrepreneurs are often struggling for guidance to identify upcoming problems, needing a type of entrepreneurial-GPS referenced in the previous chapter, as well as a mechanism to pair them with the qualified support programs or resources that will overcome the identified problems. The challenge with this hypothetical solution is that it still requires a significant amount of time to build trust before the counselor can help each entrepreneur with each problem. To fill this gap, entrepreneurs need to be in a constant incubation environment that is all around them and is within everyone they interact with. At the time of researching the communities that could support entrepreneurs, this was a challenge we couldn't initially overcome.

Taking a closer look at the community of people who supported entrepreneurs, specifically in Kansas City, we realized that most of those people were either business owners who provided services to other entrepreneurial businesses or were involved as support program vendors. Their support came naturally as their livelihood depended upon these entrepreneurial businesses. This collective support community already had most, if not all, of the relationships with entrepreneurs in the city, though each program or vendor was largely isolated from the others. The expertise garnered by the professionals working in these programs or for the vendors was an immense base of knowledge that could greatly enhance any entrepreneurial venture. Unfortunately,

"Incubators are ideal for entrepreneurs and their businesses but not feasible for a city or region due to huge investments in labor and finances. Instead of creating full-service programming within a city or region, the leaders need to enlist individuals to use their existing skills to become the incubator. This will connect the dots for entrepreneurs, keep them starting or growing their business, and direct them to the resources they need. That is an ecosystem."

~Danny Lobina

much like the entrepreneurial pods, the connectivity between these programs and vendors was limited, often to a closed loop, within the city. We knew that these programs and vendors, just like the pods, were arranged like this for the benefit of the entrepreneurs, not to restrict them. However, at the time, we could only imagine what the outcome would be if Kansas City as a metro became an interconnected pod.

Interestingly this "pod" framework proposed for Kansas City was, and still is, very similar to the entrepreneur program structures, known as entrepreneur ecosystems. Entrepreneur ecosystems are essentially a city or region-wide pod that provides some form of entrepreneur guidance along with some level of interconnected programs and vendors. These ecosystems have naturally formed over decades in cities and regions like Silicon Valley, Boston, Boulder, or Austin. As these ecosystems evolved, government, civic, and institutional leaders realized their existence and further embraced the structure; much like finding an oasis in a desert and then protecting it to ensure it continues to produce water. In these thriving entrepreneurial cities and regions, the ecosystems act as the internal economic engine which drives business creation and growth as well as the structures that are unique to each community. These cities or regions would seem to provide a blueprint, yet, we realized that these entrepreneur ecosystems were only embraced after they naturally formed. Kansas

"Building an entrepreneur ecosystem is incredibly complex with all of the moving parts, not to mention an entrepreneur population that is constantly in flux. Identifying the entrepreneur "hot spots" in the city or region and connecting with them is a good start, but the goal must be to include the entire community. Without a structured process to guide the way, government and civic leaders tend to take control of the situation and command and control the growth...which clearly doesn't work in this instance."

~ Jeff Kaczmarek

City was somewhere between the beginning and middle of that process, so we guessed we still had at least 10-15 years to wait for the natural formation of the ecosystem.

It was decided to learn what we could from the naturally-forming ecosystems, and then focus on organically accelerating the formation of an entrepreneur ecosystem. The first realization we had in researching entrepreneur ecosystems was that the support programs and vendors were largely grouped into 10 general categories. The 10 categories and their overarching focuses were:

1. Entrepreneur Feeder Program – Feeder programs help entrepreneurs find and connect with programs they may not know exist or cannot find. Entrepreneur feeder programs come as both public and private resource networks.

2. Business Training – Business training programs develop skills and knowledge that an entrepreneur must possess before starting, operating and growing a business. Business training programs are typically instructor-led curriculums in a classroom, but online courses are increasing in popularity and fit varying schedules.

3. Business Coaching – Business coaching programs connect business

"The 10 categories of programs are the resources, tools, and services entrepreneurs need to start or grow their businesses. Most cities and regions have these categories but lack a cohesive method of directing entrepreneurs to appropriate programs at the appropriate times. The community in naturally-forming ecosystems becomes the cohesive structure, while the majority of communities, cities, and regions are never able to achieve this connectivity. Both programs and connectivity are needed for success!"

~ Barry J Crocker

consultants who provide guidance, feedback and a 'sounding board' to help entrepreneurs start and grow their business. Business coaching programs can be sub-categorized into two general groups: privately owned (paid by entrepreneur) and federally funded (paid by taxpayers).

4. Resources – Resource programs connect entrepreneurs to the providers, tools and products/services needed to start and grow a business. Many entrepreneurs are unaware of what is available or how to find the right resource at the right time, so resource programs provide accessibility.

5. Mentoring – Mentoring programs pair successful entrepreneurs (mentors) with less experienced entrepreneurs (mentees). Mentors donate their time, provide insights and advice from their experiences to help the mentee avoid pitfalls and take advantage of the recommended strategies and tactics.

6. Capital – Capital programs connect entrepreneurs with private-sector investors, banks/institutions, federal grants, and other capital sources to finance startups and growing businesses.

7. Collaboration – Collaboration programs provide gathering times for entrepreneurs to share experiences and learn from each other, whether online or in-person. Collaboration is as much a learning experience for entrepreneurs as it is a means to regain motivation.

8. Entrepreneurial Events – Event programs showcase entrepreneurial businesses to the community and generate a short-duration of excitement and energy. Other forms of entrepreneurial events include and showcase; trainings, tutorials, expert speakers, and networking congregating like-minded entrepreneurs and business professionals together.

9. Business Media - Business media is actually less a program and more a platform to promote, interview or showcase startups, growing business, and their initiatives. This may be through a distribution network in print, television, radio, online blogs, social media or through a combination of initiatives.

10. Analytics - Analytic programs measure and track a business and provide entrepreneurs insights for how to overcome challenges and grow.

Each entrepreneur ecosystem is unique in how it has evolved to guide entrepreneurs through these program categories. The inherent challenge is keeping entrepreneurs focused within the ecosystem as their businesses start and grow, as ecosystems have evolved to work entrepreneurs from the idea stage to success. Ironically, the greatest threat to this focus actually comes from within the city or region as a result of the ecosystem's success. As more service providers and vendors are drawn to the ecosystem, their excitement to gain and keep more entrepreneurial customers can actu-

"Every city or region has a unique culture, business acumen, and strengths, which create unique business environments and ecosystems. What plagues community leaders is the focus on building their ecosystem into "Silicon Valley." The solution lies in fostering the positive aspects of the proverbial "Silicon Valley" into a city or region's unique and natural entrepreneur ecosystem."

~ Mark W. Dickey

"This is the ultimate conundrum for training and supporting a corporate audience vs. entrepreneurs. Traditionally, experienced experts trained and supported entrepreneurs by demonstrating a better way. With entrepreneurs and business owners, instruction needs to focus on sharing the experiences of experts so the needed skills will be self-realized and support will be sought. Thus entrepreneurship requires a new playbook and strategy, especially when accelerating the formation of an ecosystem!"

~ Jeff Kaczmarek

"This reality renders most entrepreneurial support programs and efforts ineffective. Overcoming this behavior is critical to fostering entrepreneurship and growing an economy!"

~ Danny Lobina

ally disrupt the natural flow of the ecosystem. This makes it difficult for entrepreneurs to pass through the categories and programs necessary to start or build their business.

The prospect of keeping entrepreneurs' focus is an unlikely one. Entrepreneurs become entrepreneurs to achieve their dream, be their own boss and realize their own passion. Essentially, entrepreneurs are open to help in identifying all the problems, possible answers and available solutions...but want the control to make the decisions for their business.

This reinforces Darrell's perspective that entrepreneurs are not seeking the answer, but rather an understanding of the process so they can make the decisions for their business. This critical insight also spotlights a formidable dilemma for organically accelerating an entrepreneur ecosystem, as well as for government, civic, and institutional leaders trying to maintain one: How can entrepreneurs be economically supported in a manner that generates more value than it costs? Entrepreneurs require significant amounts of time and resources to start and grow their businesses and are known to have high failure rates. It is difficult to identify how or where to invest in entrepreneurship that will deliver a good Return on Investment *(ROI)*. Additionally it was important to analyze if cities or region's have the resources to be able to provide personal attention to every entrepreneur.

Ironically, the right combination of the required guidance, programs, and vendors was only known after a city's or region's entrepreneurial ecosystem had naturally formed. Therefore, understanding which programs to prescribe into an ecosystem ahead of time was another challenge facing the prospect of organically accelerating the process. Identifying productive programs appeared to be a variation of Russian roulette, however, we did identify some constant needs that all entrepreneur ecosystems required:

1. Attracting a strong steady supply of entrepreneurs into the entrepreneur support programs.

2. Understanding that entrepreneurs don't know what they don't know, implementing a mechanism to educate them on the needs they don't know they have, and guiding them to the solutions they don't yet know they need.

"Entrepreneurship is an extremely complex profession for those involved. It is even more complex for city and county leaders trying to facilitate a revival or growth from the outside. Thus leaders seem to wait for entrepreneurship to naturally bloom and then try to identify why it happened and support it. Identifying the successful process ahead of its implementation is seemingly impossible...unless the factors impacting entrepreneurship are understood."

~ Christopher Doroh

3. Implementing a tracking mechanism to gage entrepreneurial progress so a city or region knows which support programs are most effective.

Organically accelerating an entrepreneurial ecosystem seemed infinitely complex and most likely impossible. Brad Feld was right on in his book, "Startup Communities: Building an Entrepreneurial Ecosystem in Your City," when he referenced taking a long-term, 20 year approach to build a thriving entrepreneur community, as the amount of variables and factors that would need to be simultaneously aligned to organically accelerate an ecosystem were immense!

"When a community starts to embrace the changes that develop and support entrepreneurship and calculated risk taking, a dynamic synergy develops between the community and entrepreneurs. This is a critical step to organically accelerating a city or region's natural entrepreneur ecosystem."

~ Brien M. Starner

Though in the humble opinion of the Advisory Experts and myself, most of the variables, factors, and challenges are only significant when the city's or region's community is not involved. As each community has the volunteer potential to invest the time needed to support every entrepreneur, the insights to know what programs would at least be utilized, and the will to embrace entrepreneurship much faster than the few decades it would naturally take to form. So perhaps organically accelerating entrepreneur ecosystems may actually have more to do with a community's involvement, or a city's or region's collective voice, than it does with the entrepreneurs. This perspective may likely seem absurd, but the Advisory Experts have often found this to be more true than most realize!

Think about the cities that have a naturally formed entrepreneur eco-system; e.g. Silicon Valley, Boston, or Austin. Assuming you haven't lived in one of those cities, do you personally know any entrepreneurs that have started and grown businesses there? Chances are you don't know many, if any. How many entrepreneurs from those same cities have you heard about through community blogs, conversations with residents of those cities, or from city, regional, or national news? Chances are most of us have heard of several entrepreneurs from these sources and thereby perceive those cities to be teaming with entrepreneurial activity. Thus the perception of strong entrepreneurial activity actually has more to do with the collective of voices promoting the entrepreneurial business, than it does with those entrepreneurs who are starting or growing businesses.

"Why?" you ask. Well, this points to a highly overlooked reality that economic growth is based almost completely on perceptions, whether that is with entrepreneurs or the stock market. If people perceive corporations to be strong and the economy to be stronger, then they will act by buying stocks and driving up the prices. The same applies for entrepreneurship in a city or region. If the community perceives activity and growth, people will act accordingly by becoming entrepreneurs or supporting those new and growing businesses.

> *"The idea that entrepreneurship is extremely dependent upon community involvement is a foreign thought, yet seemingly obvious. Thus, community-driven entrepreneurship provides a broad range of benefits to a city or region. This perspective truly could be a game-changer for economic development."*
>
> *~ Lisa Franklin*

Think about that for a moment. Regardless of the actual numbers of entrepreneurs or their activity in the market, most people will believe their city or region is growing or declining based on the opinions of individuals within their community. For instance, few years ago, many entrepreneurs began relocating to Silicon Valley because they perceived greater entrepreneurial opportunities there, even though Kansas City was actually experiencing an incredible number of entrepreneurial wins and thriving activity. The decades required for an entrepreneur ecosystem to naturally form are primarily needed to persuade and change the community's perspective on supporting entrepreneurship.

"This is absolutely true. If an organization never sends out communications about its services, or quits, customers will not know they existed or believe the business has closed. Thus, perceptions of people and communities are based upon the activities they read and hear about. This insight means influencing perceptions is as powerful as influencing businesses."

~ Christopher Doroh

This demonstrates that while entrepreneur ecosystems may naturally require decades to evolve, there are opportunities to organically accelerate the process if the community is onboard and engaged. It will, however, require government and civic leaders to become servant leaders for the community, meaning they need to lead the growth of entrepreneurship by supporting the community's efforts. In the next chapter, the solution to the challenges of organically accelerating the natural formation of an entrepreneur ecosystem will be addressed. Get ready to experience the method for organic acceleration, which will replace entrepreneur ecosystems, known as the Organic Environment!

Chapter 4:

Organically Accelerating Entrepreneur Ecosystems

In 2008, Joe Mullins and I started an incubator in North Kansas City *(a suburb of Kansas City)* called the Avvio Center, (startup in Italian). At the time, we thought that a physical presence was a necessity to accelerate an entrepreneur ecosystem. We got state tax credits, worked out a deal with a supportive landlord, and began accepting entrepreneur applications. Soon after we had opened and begun to work with several entrepreneurial businesses, we realized a hard lesson. The few entrepreneurs that were in the incubator were willing to come to the facility, but were specifically interested in a guidance system, or GPS, to support their efforts in starting or growing their businesses. They sought increased access to qualified support programs and vendors, as well as access to coveted promotions, events, and capital sources like investors. The community was willing to help and support the entrepreneurs but were not necessarily convinced that the Avvio Center could help entrepreneurs outside of North Kansas City. Even more frustrating was the fact that most of our time was being spent on tasks to pay the bills and were unrelated to the needs of the entrepreneurs or attracting community support.

The lesson learned was to first intimately understand the entrepreneur and the community perspectives before rushing in to provide the solution we thought best. We realized that when we could understand these two audiences, the solution to organically accelerate the entrepreneur ecosystem would become clear. We also reflected back on the questions that Larry Lee posed in Chapter 2, and we realized that he was posing the questions that would lead us to the answer.

"To truly support entre-preneurship in a way that can grow an entire community's economy requires an acute understanding of the factors impacting entrepreneurship and the community."

~ Christopher Doroh

While formulating the Organic Environment, I was fascinated by how a few entrepreneurs built successful ventures and did so repeatedly, while most entrepreneurs failed. I reached out to these successful entrepreneurs across the country and in multiple industries to discover what they attributed their successes to. It often took several beers before they would describe their successful process, stressing that it was just their personal approach. After roughly 50 meetings, Steve Meinzen and I analyzed the results and had a shocking revelation…across the country and across industries - all of these successful entrepreneur processes were nearly identical! They had independently realized the same process that actually worked best to consistently develop successful businesses.

"Entrepreneurship, from an outside perspective, looks like a game of chance. But at its core, business creation and growth is a fairly systematic process. This is proven by the multitude of repeat entre-preneurs who have succeeded using eerily similar methods."

~ Danny Lobina

This revelation was monumental! However, it came with an equally monumental challenge: how could entrepreneurs be trained on the process? We knew entrepreneurs started their own businesses specifically to be their own boss and make their own independent decisions. So why would an entrepreneur utilize training that would infringe on that territory? And would they perceive a proven startup and growth process to be better than their own? Additionally would cities and regions be willing to provide the resources, investors, coaches, and mentors necessary for the process?

At this point, I was ready to go back to the 50 entrepreneurs to ask for clarity when Steve, a serial entrepreneur himself, pointed out that the answers to the previous questions needed to be understood first-hand. Steve suggested that we quit dancing around the problem by searching for insights and dive right in to understand each perspective for ourselves. Steve also pointed out that the best way to figure out how to organically accelerate an ecosystem, as well as how to incentivize resources, investors, coaches and mentors into the process, was simply to figure it out first-hand in Kansas City.

Following Steve's advice, I decided to use the process from the 50 entrepreneurs to figure out the secret to entrepreneur success. To achieve this I needed to understand exactly how entrepreneurs are supported at each stage in starting or growing their business. I began to organize entrepreneur events, hold small group sessions, host mentoring and coaching meetings for entrepreneurs, host business conferences, and launch investor forums. All this was done to gain the first-hand understanding for how entrepreneurs interacted and benefited from investors, mentors, coaches, fellow entrepreneurs, and others within their city or region.

After nearly four years of immersing myself in entrepreneurial activity and using all of the research discussed in the previous chapters, I observed:

A. Entrepreneurs constantly experience roadblocks in starting or building their businesses.

B. Events, conferences, and small groups provide short-term clarity and progress for entrepreneurs facing the roadblocks, but there seems to be a gap where a long-term solution should be.

C. Mentors, investors, coaches and even resource providers are interested in helping startup entrepreneurs for the potential of future financial gain, but have difficulty connecting with entrepreneurs and their businesses at the appropriate time.

D. Structured events bring investors, mentors, and coaches together with entrepreneurs in a context that allows productivity, which is often lacking in chance meetings. *(Though again, events are like fireworks; they create a flash of excitement and then quickly fade out of mind.)*

E. Entrepreneurs constantly re-evaluate their strategy after interacting with those they trust or respect, which may cause constant tweaks or changes to their entrepreneurial and business direction. *(These changes and tweaks are much more significant in startups than for growing businesses.)*

F. Support programs, and vendors are often operated independently or are isolated from complementary programs and vendors. Entrepreneurs are often burdened by having to forge and build a relationship every time they have a need, rather than having a 1-stop shop for support that is interconnected throughout the city or region.

G. Family, friends, and acquaintances (who have little knowledge of entrepreneurship but live or work in close proximity to an entrepreneur), investors, mentors, coaches, or support vendors can be highly influential in their decisions. Thus it isn't solely a business community that affects entrepreneurship, but everyone within a city or region, as their opinions and actions are constantly shaping the environment of creating and growing businesses.

I also met many people, regarded as leaders by their peers, who at first glance had similar observations. These people were investors, entrepreneurs, mentors, resource providers, coaches who were collectively involved in entrepreneurship. Each of their observations were based on their unique perspectives, experiences, and interactions with the entrepreneur environment. Ultimately their observations were focused around a strategy each believed would help or support entrepreneurial businesses more efficiently and effectively. Each of these people had observed entrepreneurship from a specific viewpoint, and their observations and resulting strategies reflected that. However, after aggregating these observations and the resulting strategies together, the outcome hinted at a revolutionary approach. This approach could be the comprehensive process for how to support entrepreneurs at an intimate level while still being scalable for the masses. The approach could engage and involve an entire community in a manner that would increase the speed and magnitude of success.

"Solving the entrepreneurship and economic equations is rooted in collaboration. As societies are built by large groups of diverse people, so too are economies. A workable economic process will incorporate strategies from a multitude of focuses, programs, and experts. Entrepreneurship and economic success must be tied to a fully integrated system or ecosystem."

~ Mark W. Dickey

"Entrepreneurship in Kansas City is continually grown by entrepreneurs and the support of the community. It's interesting that those two same audiences had to work together to spark the growth. This collaboration requires a strategy, much more than a simple program or incubator, that can deliver incredible results.

~ Lisa Franklin

This led to the following discovery: The true potential of entrepreneurship in Kansas City and other cities and regions can only be realized when there is simultaneous support and engagement from 1) the community AND 2) the entrepreneurs. Think back to the exercise conducted at the end of Chapter 3, when you were asked to identify how you heard of the most prominent entrepreneurial cities. That exercise emphasized the equal value that a community shares with entrepreneurs in achieving a strong and growing economy in a city or region.

This revelation meant that focusing on helping Kansas City's community understand, embrace, and promote entrepreneurship was as important as creating and building the entrepreneurial businesses. Fast forward 7 years and the revelation to dually focus on entrepreneurs and the community became the key that led to increased entrepreneurial and economic growth in Kansas City, Blue Springs, Lee's Summit, and Moberly.

Therefore, the Organic Environment methodology behind *The Organic Entrepreneur Economy* first focuses on understanding how a community and entrepreneurs think and act, referred to as the **Social Infrastructures**, and only then focuses on a solution to growing entrepreneurship and the community through operational strategies, referred to as the **Operational Infrastructures**. In the Organic Environment methodology the entrepreneurs and the community both have a corresponding social and operational infrastructure. The four infrastructures, each discussed in an upcoming chapter, will help government and civic leaders understand entrepreneurs and the community, and will guide the implementation of operations and actions to organically accelerate the economy and decrease the time it takes to form an otherwise naturally-forming entrepreneur ecosystem.

"Physical Infrastructures provide the groundwork for commerce and economic potential in any city or region. These four "human" Infrastructures provide a new kind of groundwork to allow for exponential commerce and economic potential in the post-Great Recession economy."

~ Lisa Franklin

Here is an overview of the four infrastructures:

1. **Entrepreneur Social Infrastructure** – Understanding what causes entrepreneurs to start or grow businesses, and how to motivate them.

2. **Community Social Infrastructure** – Understanding what causes a collective of people, referred to as a community, to support entrepreneurs and their businesses, as well as what motivates the community to take action.

3. **Community Operational Infrastructure** – Leveraging the community and entrepreneur social infrastructures to implement operational strategies to grow a supportive community, innovative culture, and community volunteers that support the operations needed to foster growth in entrepreneurship.

4. **Entrepreneur Operational Infrastructure** – Leveraging the entrepreneur and community social infrastructures, and community operational infrastructure to form an operational strategy that accelerates the mass creation and growth of entrepreneurial ventures throughout a city or region.

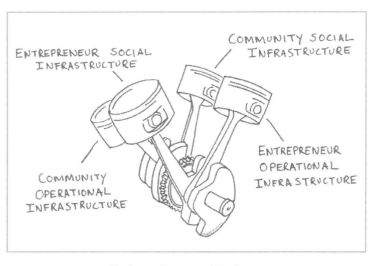

The Organic Environment's V-4 Engine:
the four infrastructures integrate to create an economic engine for the city or region

When a city or region utilizes the four infrastructures, the Organic Environment *(and thus The Organic Entrepreneur Economy)* will become their economic engine. Just as a high performance V-4 engine is a favorite for Formula 1 racing teams, with 4 precision pistons that pump up and down to turn the crank providing power to accelerate rapidly, so too the four infrastructures will operate to accelerate and drive the economy forward.

Every engine is different - just as every city or region is different - so the four infrastructures are adaptable and customizable. It is also important to understand how the engine that is running an economy works, so it can be fixed when it slows down or breaks. Critical to success are the driver and controls connected to the engine that initiates the acceleration and forward momentum at the right moment. The Organic Environment and the four Infrastructures provide both the understanding on how the engine is running and the controls that effectively operate the economic engine. *(While not included in this book: The Organic Entrepreneur Economy, there is a user's manual for the economic engine, or Organic Environment and four infrastructures, that is available separately for government and civic leaders or anyone interested in "mechanically" tuning their economy!)*

"The "human component" in supporting entrepreneurship, or how people and their opinions are involved, is often forgotten. Leaders forget that entrepreneurial businesses are led by people who are passionate about their business. Thus it should be much more of an emotional support process."

~ Michie P. Slaughter

You have probably noticed that *The Organic Entrepreneur Economy* has not mentioned anything about the standard economic development tools, like laws, incentives *(i.e. tax credits)*, and physical infrastructures. And you are right. We recognize the significant role these tools play in the types of businesses that can be attracted to an area or the methods of commerce that are possible. However, these "tools" are not a determinant for the existence of entrepreneurship or an ecosystem, but rather are a "multiplier" for how successful a business or economy can be. The focus of the book is not on these economic development tools, but instead on the Organic Environment methodology and four infrastructures that will determine the development of a growing economy by utilizing the entrepreneurs and community in a city or region. This approach will ultimately offer government and civic leaders the insights to know which economic development tools to implement to multiply their already growing economy!

"Government and civic leaders tend to focus too much on tools and initiatives and forget how important the social mindsets, business culture or the people are to their community and building a thriving Organic Environment for entrepreneurs."

~ Brien M. Starner

The Organic Entrepreneur Economy's Organic Environment methodology and four infrastructures were recognized, by the Advisory Experts, to be the answer for organically accelerating the formation of a naturally forming entrepreneur ecosystem, rapidly foster entrepreneurship, a supportive community and culture, resulting in faster economic growth. The only milestone left at this point was to build the Organic Environment and the four infrastructures into the cities and regions that needed them. So we did. Along the way we realized that the most effective, efficient, and sustainable approach to implementing the Organic Environment was through facilitation from government and civic leaders and frontline implementation by those within the community. An overview of *The Organic Entrepreneur Economy*'s Organic Environment methodology and four infrastructures are showcased in the corresponding diagram to provide a preview of what will be discussed in the following chapters.

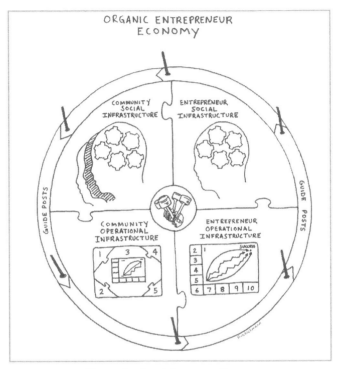

The complete *Organic Entrepreneur Economy*:
Organic Environment, four Infrastructures and 6 Guideposts

Chapter 5:

The Entrepreneur Social Infrastructure

I have seen many Kansas City entrepreneurs enroll in mentoring, coaching or training programs to gain answers or insights, and watched as many still struggle with how to apply those insights into their businesses. I remember working with an entrepreneur named Travis Bowring whose business, Rippin' Fish, connected fishing guides with clients seeking an expedition with a guaranteed catch of fish. Travis had received mentoring and coaching on how to use social media to attract customers, but regularly got stuck and confused when attempting to apply this knowledge. Travis understood the insights in theory, but found it difficult to execute since he lacked the base of experience that the mentors and coaches possessed. Travis is not alone. I have interviewed dozens of entrepreneurs about this very challenge, and nearly all of them struggled with executing insights they had not personally experienced. This situation is like a novice who is skydiving for the first time alone after watching a video on how and when to open the parachute. It is just not enough!

Entrepreneurs that do not have the experiences to identify how the advice of coaches and mentors is relevant to their business or how to apply it, they are missing the context. In order for entrepreneurs to be helped and supported by successful entrepreneurs, mentors, coaches, and the community, government and civic leaders, these very helpers need to understand how entrepreneurs think, perceive the more experienced people around them, and apply the knowledge they obtain. It is with this understanding, that community, government and civic leaders can utilize the Organic Environment to actively foster and support entrepreneurship.

"It's rare to find a visionary and a doer in today's business environment. Entrepreneurs must be both! Communities must learn that each entrepreneur is different and they may not "fit" into a "canned" program. Communities must take time to learn the needs of each entrepreneur and provide customized programming to ensure their success."

~Corey J. Mehaffy

The career of an entrepreneur is unlike any other. It is not a profession requiring a degree or certificate or book knowledge. Understanding how an entrepreneur has been trained is often a mystery. The path to becoming successful is as diverse as the personalities of those involved. This makes it difficult to understand how entrepreneurs start and build businesses, or why they are hesitant to listen to the insights, directions, or suggested actions of other experienced entrepreneurs. The resulting randomness of success makes it is easy to understand why government and civic leaders struggle to understand their role in supporting these businesses.

A person cannot expect to be taken seriously by randomly walking off the street, entering a job site, and offering pertinent suggestions on how to complete a project faster. In the same way, government and civic leaders struggle with whether and how to advise entrepreneurs. Interestingly entrepreneurs evaluate advice and take actions in similar ways, called **mindsets**. These mindsets are usually subconscious, meaning entrepreneurs aren't intentionally thinking this way, although they usually realize the validity of the mindsets when asked. Similarly the Evis Consulting team, Advisory Experts and I recognized the presence of these mindsets in our past entrepreneurial endeavors, and thus have put these into practice to help government and civic leaders understand and support entrepreneurs.

In 2009, Kansas City was the test bed for the refinement of these mindsets, as we needed to understand how entrepreneurs learn and make decisions if we wished to provide a structure that offered support and guidance on their terms. As a result, I co-created an event called 'Just for Starters' with fellow entrepreneurs from the KC roundtable, an entrepreneurial group I had recently co-founded. 'Just for Starters' was an opportunity for a live audience to watch six entrepreneurs individually present their businesses and answer questions from a panel comprising an investor, a mentor, and a successful entrepreneur who was a CEO for his/her business. The result was an inside look into how entrepreneurs were starting and growing their businesses, as well as a perspective for how these entrepreneurs perceived and utilized insights from others.

"To understand how to foster a strong and diverse base of entrepreneurs, it is imperative to understand how business owners think, act, and behave. Knowing this will provide the necessary perspectives for supporting and attracting the entrepreneurial masses to your city or region's economy."

~ Mark W. Dickey

We used this information to refocus our efforts. Kansas City entrepreneurs no longer grew businesses below the radar. Instead, they became our friends and colleagues who regularly asked for our support. I like to compare this to the Blue Whale migration patterns that were a mystery, but which are now understood. Whales can now found and studied throughout their lifecycle as never before. These mindsets were shared with Jeff Kaczmarek, President of the Kansas City Economic Development Corporation at the time, who utilized the insights to engage with these formerly elusive entrepreneurs and businesses.

> *"The conundrum for entrepreneurs is knowing when to listen and when to act. Not listening to others' advice probably created the startup or business in the first place. But not listening in the first 5 years after launch is the greatest cause of failure."*
>
> *~ Michie P. Slaughter*

The five mindsets comprised within the Entrepreneurial Social Infrastructure provided the clarity into how entrepreneurs think, their instincts (or subconscious evaluations of situations), and their actions. These five mindsets will later be put into practice in the Entrepreneur Operational Infrastructure, which will be discussed in Chapter 8. The five mindsets within the Entrepreneur Social Infrastructure are:

1. **Perception**

2. **Context**

3. **Experiential Learning**

4. **Perceived Control of Free Will**

5. **Needs vs. Wants Paradigm**

A clear understanding each of these five mindsets will provide government and civic leaders the necessary understanding for how to support their startup and growing entrepreneurial businesses. The following sections explain each mindset in greater detail to clarify how to better engage and support entrepreneurs in a given city or region.

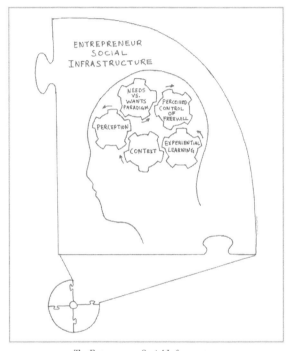

The Entrepreneur Social Infrastructure:
the 5 mindsets that drive the entrepreneur's thoughts and actions

Mindset 1: Perception

"Science is nothing but perception" ~ *Plato*

Perception is the first and base mindset for the Entrepreneur Social Infrastructure upon which the other mindsets are born. It is also the single most powerful mindset that guides entrepreneurs in their decision-making and actions, since it dictates how they interpret their experiences, interactions, and environment.

"Entrepreneurs are people who come into this "profession" with unique backgrounds and experiences. Thus each will perceive a similar situation in their own way. The result of this reality is that each entrepreneur must be approached and supported differently. The perception mindset explains how to overcome this situation when targeting entrepreneurs."

~ *Danny Lobina*

To this point Barry Crocker, serial entrepreneur and Partner at Evis Consulting, observed that entrepreneurs perceive that any time spent away from their business is wasted. In actuality, time spent on training, mentoring insights, or networking are actually investments into their business and themselves. Barry's roles in mentoring many, many businesses has provided him with first-hand experience into how perceptions can be so different, even when entrepreneurs are receiving the same advice at the same time. Barry says that entrepreneur's perceptions drive the formation of their own businesses, as well as their suggestions to other entrepreneurs.

To apply Barry's perspective, if a small group of entrepreneurs perceive that support programs and vendors in a city are lacking or ineffective, they will look for support vendors and programs outside of their city or region, and will encourage others to do the same. The irony here is that this small group of entrepreneurs may be inaccurate in their assessment or difficult customers to work with, but they will still send the message of lacking or ineffective support to other entrepreneurs. Entrepreneurial perceptions can easily and quickly cause a chain reaction that is counterproductive to a city or region...but they can also create chains of super productive activity as well!

Early in my development of Kansas City entrepreneurs, I came across Mark Manley, leader of the Small Business Technology Development Center at the University of Central Missouri, who wrote patents for entrepreneurs. Mark would write patents, as a patent agent, at a reduced cost to entrepreneurs, thus saving them thousands of dollars. Unfortunately, very few people ever took advantage of his service. When asking entrepreneurs who actually needed patents why they were not utilizing this service, I discovered: 1) influential entrepreneurs were not promoting Mark as a trusted source of patents, 2) there was a perception that only attorneys wrote the best patents, and 3) most entrepreneurs who need a patent check with other entrepreneurs for referrals. These entrepreneurial perceptions may not have been based on fact, but they might as well have been, as this was keeping entrepreneurs from engaging in a valuable resource. Once Mark was aware of these perceptions, he and his staff could act accordingly and increase their attractiveness to entrepreneurs by focusing on their perceptions.

Here is a simple guide for understanding the perceptions that drive an entrepreneur's thoughts, decisions, and actions:

1. Perceptions are unique to each entrepreneur.

2. An entrepreneur's perceptions define fact and fiction in their minds.

3. Perceived facts are the basis for any decisions, whether emotional or business.

4. Decisions lead to actions.

"Understanding how entrepreneurs think is critical when identifying how they start and grow businesses and how they want and need to be helped. This will also be beneficial for understanding how to effectively engage with entrepreneurs."

~ Christopher Doroh

An entrepreneur's decision to start a business or whom he picks to ask for help stems from what they perceive to be true. To understand an entrepreneur's perception is to understand how they will come to a decision and act. The value of perceptions is translated into a staple exercise at corporate retreats through the 'trust fall'. In the 'trust fall' a person climbs a ladder and then has to fall back and trust that they will be caught by those behind or beneath him/her. The person's decision to fall backwards is predicated on the perception of whether the 'catchers' are to be trusted. So too, entrepreneurs must perceive support programs and services to be trustworthy before taking the leap of faith to engage with them.

Establishing a perception of trust will be further explained and utilized within the four additional mindsets:

- Context
- Experiential Learning
- Perceived Control of Free Will
- Needs vs. Wants Paradigm

These mindsets provide insights into the struggles entrepreneurs have in perceiving clarity (Context), perceiving the next steps of development for their business (Experiential Learning), perceiving control of all facets of their business (Perceived Control of Free Will), and perceiving what is actually needed to achieve business success (Needs vs. Wants Paradigm). It is important to remember that entrepreneurs' perceptions are in a constant state of flux, as each experience and interaction they have is altering their perspective. So while understanding each mindset is important, keeping up-to-date with the entrepreneurs' perceptions in your city or region is equally as important, even if challenging.

Perceptions often evolve or are based primarily on interactions with trusted advisors and fellow entrepreneurs. These trusted advisors who exert influence are referred to as **influencers**. Once influencers' opinions are perceived by entrepreneurs to be credible, many future business decisions will be based upon that advice. This makes locating and finding entrepreneurial influencers very important for an entrepreneur, and even more important for the community, as these influencers could be a critical determinant to the success of a startup or growing business.

"Entrepreneurs' perceptions are based on the information they gather from others, media, and their environment. These perceptions direct their views, actions, and decision making. This motivator seems straightforward, but since the information entrepreneurs receive is constantly changing, their actions and decisions are also in flux. This constant evolution makes it very difficult to predict the behavior of entrepreneurs when attempting to support their business creation or growth efforts."

~ Barry J Crocker

Locating influencers can be difficult, but here are some common sources: national and regional entrepreneurial bloggers, business publications, news broadcasts and professional conferences. Perhaps the best strategy for finding influencers,

> *"Influencing perceptions, without being forceful, is the key to change. This type of influence is necessary to provide support and guidance to entrepreneurs."*
>
> *~ Danny Lobina*

however, is simply to identify who is offering to help entrepreneurs in your city or region. Understanding how these influencers are supporting entrepreneurs, government and civic leaders (as well as the community) can learn how to guide this powerful interaction. This concept of influencing entrepreneurs is discussed in greater detail in the following chapters.

Whether government or civic leaders are seeking to foster entrepreneur creation, incubate new businesses, or accelerate growth in existing businesses, knowledge of the entrepreneurs' perceptions and who their influencers are is fundamental. This knowledge will provide the insights for how to approach and support entrepreneurs in the community. The more government and civic leaders understand about entrepreneurs' perceptions, the more their unpredictable actions will become...predictable.

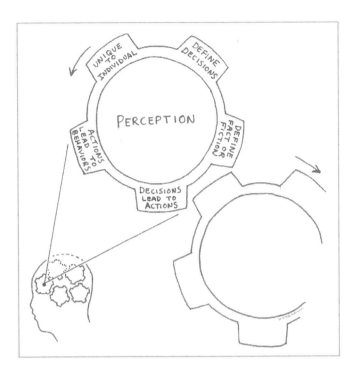

The Perception Mindset

Mindset 2: Context

"One simply cannot fully understand the value of advice, without first experiencing it." ~ Unknown

Context relates to the relevant knowledge or experiences entrepreneurs use to understand a situation, interaction or communication. This is important as entrepreneurs are constantly being bombarded with information, but they cannot take appropriate action until they have comprehended the intended meaning of that information. When a person asks for directions in a foreign country and receives them in a foreign language, he/she does not have the appropriate knowledge to understand those directions. Similarly when attempting to provide entrepreneurs with answers to grow their businesses, mentors and coaches sometimes provide answers that aren't understood correctly or at all.

"The Context Mindset addresses the greatest challenge when supporting entrepreneurs. Entrepreneurs often struggle to comprehend the intention of advice or direction. This happens all the time and will often go undetected until there is a negative result. This mindset depicts critical information that is needed by all program or support personnel attempting to help entrepreneurs."

~ Danny Lobina

Context is the "intended understanding" needed to interpret and then act upon communicated information. It is critical for government and civic leaders to understand the importance of context, as it redefines how to support entrepreneurs. Leaders must not simply provide the right resource, solution or answer. Instead, the focus needs to be on how the entrepreneur is able to come to the "right" or "intended" context, as well as to understand when context has been lost. Only when the entrepreneur understands the correct context, will access to the intended support be perceived as beneficial. It is also important to realize that understanding context is not a skill, but an evolving base of knowledge that entrepreneurs and government/civic leaders alike must garner to better achieve context.

For example, John Wendorff, the owner of The Personal Marketing Company, is a successful real estate printing entrepreneur who has overcome some significant challenges related to context as he built his impressive business. John has become a mentor for new businesses and young entrepreneurs, and his style is to pose questions that force the entrepreneur to investigate his/her business and markets further. John suggests that this approach helps him, as a mentor, gain a greater understanding of the problem, as well as providing entrepreneurs with trouble shooting questions that often lead them to an answer. With John's support, the entrepreneur is able to work through his problem, as well as understand each other's context through continued dialogue.

Context is used primarily in two forms: situational or communicational. Situational context is understanding what the environment is telling you about the situation. For example, if you walk into a meeting where everyone is sitting classroom

> *"The most successful entrepreneurs are able to learn from their experiences to identify where opportunities are. The opposite of this is the "Maze Dull" entrepreneurs who can't identify trends in their experiences. The "Context Gap" points to a real struggle for entrepreneurs, as it is much more difficult to identify trends when the experiences are being put through an advisor's perspective filter."*
>
> *~ Michie P. Slaughter*

style facing a projection screen in the front, you know that someone is likely going to make a presentation. Communicational context is having to accurately interpret shared information. John mentors by posing questions, probing the entrepreneur's understanding of the questions as well as how to find the answers; this is proper use of context. In most cases, entrepreneurs do not have the contextual knowledge to understand what to do and what to avoid from this advice.

It is important to identify if support programs and vendor interactions are providing the desired insights to entrepreneurs. Entrepreneurs may not understand the context, and the result is that their actions do not match those advised. This gap, referred to as the **context gap**, disrupts entrepreneurial development and business growth. In this case, the advice-giver is likely to perceive the entrepreneur to be uncoachable, and similarly the entrepreneur is likely to perceive the advice-giver as unknowledgeable, even though both acted with the best of intentions. Identifying a context gap is important for government and civic leaders, their community, and other support services to understand. The context gap helps indicate to government and civic leaders when entrepreneurs, often in mass, are stuck or are in need of help...often even before the entrepreneur realizes it.

Early on in developing Kansas City's experience, I saw entrepreneurs

"Entrepreneurs are greatly aided by the insights of others. Occasionally entrepreneurs do not correctly understand what was advised, as they have not had sufficient experience in the industry or market. This "Context Gap" is disruptive to entrepreneurs but rarely identified. Realizing and addressing this miscommunication enhances entrepreneurial outcomes."

~ Steve Meinzen

desperately reaching out to successful businessmen to gain insights on how to save or grow their business. The businessmen did their best to describe solutions and ideas, however, entrepreneurs almost always came out of those meeting as confused as before. Either the entrepreneur did not have the experience necessary to understand the advice, or the mentor had difficulty understanding the problem or context and offered a misappropriate answer. When working with cities to grow their entrepreneur base, I regularly encounter a context gap with government and civic leaders who lack the experience needed to understand and support entrepreneurs. This context gap often leaves leaders unsure about how to help entrepreneurs reach their goals.

Mentoring programs and the personnel attempting to supplement entrepreneurs' limited experiences are also often falling victim to the context gap. The phrase "entrepreneurs don't know, what they don't know" highlights how the context gap can actually imprison an entrepreneur. Entrepreneurs often know there is something hindering their business success but don't know what it is or how to ask for help. This is a common point of failure that far too often ruins startups.

"Large-scale city or regional endeavors require constant calibration. Without it, there cannot be a realistic expectation of success in the modern world."

~ Matthew Hart

"There is not an "easy fix" to overcome the Context Gap. Asking the entrepreneur to restate their understanding or polling their comprehension is one good method for identifying any inconsistencies. Understanding this mindset is half the battle to ensuring it does not become a problem."

~ Danny Lobina

A simple strategy to overcome context misconceptions and gaps is to ask or poll entrepreneurs on what advice they gained from a situation or training. This provides an opportunity to identify if context is an issue. Once it is determined that perceptions are in line with the intended communication or environment, it is important to again ask how he/she might put the advice, situation or training into practice. This helps ensure that the entrepreneur has the relevant knowledge and experience to take productive action, and if not, provides an opportunity to supplement their understanding.

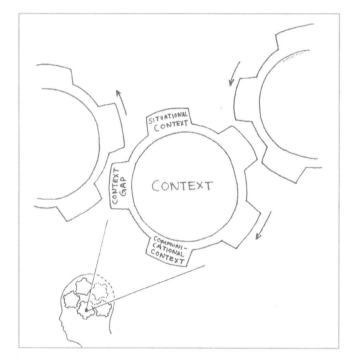

The Context Mindset

Mindset 3: Experiential Learning

"The only source of knowledge is experience."
~ Albert Einstein

Learning by experiencing success and failure is a natural process of self-discovery. When a person decides to start his own business, learning will primarily be through his or her experiences. This is evident, as those who have attempted multiple business ventures - 'serial entrepreneurs' - have proven models for starting and growing businesses that they have learned along the way and then use with a high-degree of success going forward. These models have and are constantly being refined over time through trial and error.

As earlier research in this book showed, serial entrepreneurs from across the United States have all arrived at strikingly similar models for how to achieve entrepreneurial success. Though each considered his model to be unique due to personal trials and errors, the models from nearly 50 serial entrepreneurs were all eerily similar. This indicates that there is a best practice for guiding one through trial and error to effectively start up or grow a business. It also indicates that most entrepreneurs will need to startup and grow several businesses before

> *"Experience is critical for entrepreneurs to be successful! Serially successful entrepreneurs have usually been serially unsuccessful at some point in their career. So the focus is how to guide entrepreneurs to success without having a catastrophic business failure. This is incredibly valuable to entrepreneurs and to an economy, as it is essentially a shortcut to short and long-term success."*
>
> *~ Danny Lobina*

they will naturally learn the same lessons as the serial entrepreneurs.

Since entrepreneurs learn through experiences, mentors, coaches, and training programs could better engage entrepreneurs with this in mind. Simply providing answers may seem like the obvious approach for supporting entrepreneurs, we know from the perception and context mindsets that entrepreneurs will not likely understand or accept these answers. On the other hand, if situations are suggested that guide entrepreneurs to self-realize these answers, entrepreneurs will become engaged and the perception and context mindsets will play to the trainer's advantage.

"Experiential Design is a process that was modeled after my futurist consulting. It involves experientially modeling the successful behavior and skills of entrepreneurs, and then creating a roadmap of the experiences that other entrepreneurs need to achieve success in their business. While complex, the results provide entrepreneurs with the innate understanding and skills they need to achieve greater success!"

~ Dr. Bernard Franklin

To construct these situations requires what we call **experiential design,** an approach and process for paring the learning of desired skills, traits, and insights with experiences that allow the entrepreneur to self-realize the desired answers. Additionally experiential design identifies how to organize these experiences in rapid succession, allowing the learning situations to build on top of each other. Just as in the natural process of starting or growing a business, an entrepreneur is faced with unfamiliar problems which he then attempts through trial and error to find solutions for. Experiential design can organize situational experiences in a way that illustrates how best to start or grow a business. Experiential design is about laying out the desired experiences, and then layering in coaching and mentoring engagements to guide the entrepreneur, when needed, to come to the right conclusions. More specifics on experiential learning and experiential design will be discussed in later chapters.

For example a good friend of mine named Brian Morgan, never graduated college. Though Brian's companies - OEM Services and Lampein Laboratories - are considered to be strong and beneficial businesses for Kansas City and the region. Brian jokingly admits that he has a Doctorate from the University of Hard Knocks, and has learned what he knows through trial and error. As Brian was one of the 50 entrepreneurs that we interviewed, he has figured out first-hand how to identify and overcome challenges. Brian has also mentioned on multiple occasions that

"The struggle for strictly learning out of a book or in a classroom is that entrepreneurs will have to recognize and apply the knowledge in an infinite number of other situations. This is something that is difficult for first-time entrepreneurs all the way up to the most serially-experienced entrepreneurs."

~Michie P. Slaughter

helping entrepreneurs to experience challenging situations will provide them insights that can be applied directly into their businesses. Though Brian has always pondered that the difficulty in helping entrepreneurs is to identify which problem they are on and what past experiences they are using to try to find the answer.

This is likely a struggle for government and civic leaders as well, being that it's nearly impossible to identify or keep track of the learning experiences that each entrepreneur has had or currently requires. For government and civic leaders, it must feel like having a city or region of entrepreneurial students who are progressing through an education system where the grade levels, curriculums, and test scores are invisible. This makes it very difficult to identify the phase of business an entrepreneur is in, it also points to an area where entrepreneurs are constantly struggling. Entrepreneurs are unable to see their progress and are in need of guidance. Government and civic leaders are prone to provide it, but they struggle to appropriately create the matches.

The importance of experiential design and the experiential learning mindset, building on an entrepreneurs' past experiences, will guide how they approach starting or growing a business. Understanding the past experiences of each entrepreneur will provide insights into how they strategize to reach business goals. Entrepreneurs working in similar industries will have similar experiences relating to the industry, so their approaches and strategies will also be similar. This insight will help government and civic leaders understand how entrepreneurs behave by uncovering how and what they have experienced, especially if they work in similar industries. Reviewing this behavior can help to identify if greater knowledge would help city and regional businesses become more effective and competitive, as well as understanding that effective training of entrepreneurs is

> *"An entrepreneur's inner compass, or gut instinct, is based on his/her past experiences. The design of this mindset depicts the learning that guides entrepreneurs' actions. This provides insights to effectively train entrepreneurs, as well as how to effectively guide their businesses through creation and growth. This mindset was formerly a "trade secret" of highly successful entrepreneurs."*
>
> *~ Steve Meinzen*

built on experiential design.

This mindset will greatly help government and civic leaders as they learn how to operationally support entrepreneurs in later chapters. An understanding of how entrepreneurs are learning, will enable leaders to recognize learning opportunities and when a business is struggling with a context gap. This will also help leaders to identify "warning signs" concerning the actions and behaviors of entrepreneurs. The experiences of serial entrepreneurs help them to overcome more and more context gaps, as well as constantly evolve their perceptions.

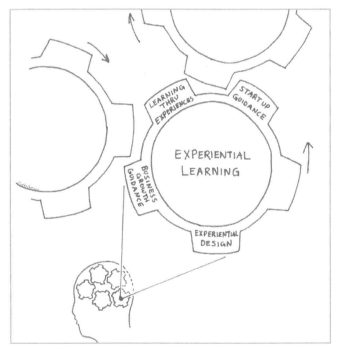

The Experiential Learning Mindset

Mindset 4: Perceived Control of Free Will

"Free will is an illusion. People will always choose the perceived path of greatest pleasure." ~ Scott Adams

It may seem that an entrepreneur is the textbook example of someone who has the utmost control of free will. However, entrepreneurs do not always perceive it that way. Many believe they are in a constant struggle to keep control during the startup and growth phases of their business. Perception of control of free will is the greatest strength and weakness of any entrepreneur. It is their strength in times of high risk, as it allows them to make quick, strategic decisions since there is no need to check with superiors for approval. On the flip side, entrepreneurs may fight so hard to keep control from motivated employees or business partners that they stunt or even destroy their businesses in the process. Often this struggle can happen in an entrepreneur's own head, as they fight the fear of what will happen by bringing motivated employees into their business. The perception of the control of free will may even become a built-in defense mechanism for entrepreneurs who have experienced repeated setbacks caused by a perception of trusting others too much with decision-making power.

"Free will in entrepreneurship is another big one! Entrepreneurs consider free will a constant, not optional. For them to continue to invest their time and money, they must perceive control of their business and its decisions. The challenge when offering guidance is to influence a change in direction, while keeping the perception that it is the entrepreneur who decides. This is an important mindset to understand!"

~ Danny Lobina

To clarify, free will is freedom to make choices and decisions as one pleases. Most entrepreneurs want control because they believe in their ability to make the best decisions for success. This belief in their abilities is likely what started the business in the first place, so there is definitely merit and value in their belief. There are others who are good at decentralizing power and not in need of being in control at all times, but these entrepreneurs are in the minority. It is widely accepted that entrepreneurs are driven by control of decision-making, or more importantly, perceiving they are in control. As an example, entrepreneurs seeking additional capital are loathe to give up controlling interest *(more than 50%)* to investors, even if it means losing personal economic rewards. An entrepreneur may become less driven or even opt to leave the company if he perceives limitations on his control or decision-making.

A major factor in choosing mentors, coaches, resource services, programs, and even business location has to do with whether these decisions will threaten or strengthen the entrepreneur's perception of their control of free will. This is often the case when entrepreneurs suddenly disengage from mentors, coaches, or training programs, as they have likely perceived that they are no longer in control. Therefore, when working with entrepreneurs, it is important to ensure that all interactions pass

> *"Entrepreneurs are often taking significant risks with their personal and family's financial future. Maintaining control of their business and making their own critical business decisions is necessary for financial risks to be perceived as worthwhile. So entrepreneurs must perceive control, even when others are offering guidance or support services."*
>
> *~ Barry J Crocker*

the '*perceived control of free will test*' to ensure the business owner remains engaged with the services and assistance they need.

The 'perceived control of free will test' includes the actions that government and civic leaders take to bolster an entrepreneur's perceived control when engaging or interacting with their businesses. The leaders can:

1. Offer greater access to advice from successful entrepreneurs

2. Offer greater access to business, financial, and employee resources

3. Offer to help by making introductions to mentors or advisors

4. Suggest success stories of entrepreneurs who controlled their own business development when working with the city or region

Conversely here are some actions that may cause entrepreneurs to perceive a loss of control:

1. An authoritative figure becomes involved and appears to supersede the entrepreneur's decisions (either in the eyes of the entrepreneur or his subordinates)

2. Undermining or trying to control the process for any of the four examples in the 'perceived control of free will test'

3. Inserting anyone or any environment that diminishes the entrepreneur's passion or drive

That last point, in particular, may seem like walking through a minefield blindfolded. However, this is where the previous mindsets really start to come into play: perception, context, and experiential learning. When the experiential learning and context mindsets are operating in conjunction with the perceived control of free will mindset, droves of entrepreneurs will be attracted because they believe that each development in their business is an organic discovery process leading them to greater success. Better yet, the resulting praise will be directed to the community, government and civic leaders for being such amazing partners in helping the entrepreneurs achieve success.

Larry Lee, the Director for the Center of Innovation and Entrepreneurship at Northwest Missouri State University, regularly confronts this perception. Entrepreneurs come to him and the center seeking guidance and support for their startup or growing business, but at the same time want to be able to make all of the decisions. While Larry may find this difficult, you would never know it by interacting with him and his team...as they effortlessly work with entrepreneurs to troubleshoot their problems and then provide solution options. The entrepreneurs then pick the solution or combination of solutions they believe are best for their business. Entrepreneurs always perceive they are in control, and most importantly, leave with a solution they believe they self-realized with the help of Larry Lee and the Center of Innovation and Entrepreneurship. The

"Entrepreneurs own businesses to have creative freedom, be in control, and do things their own way. Removing or threatening that control often causes an immediate and aggressive response. (Just as removing a corporate employee's paycheck or benefits destroys loyalty.) Fortifying or increasing an entrepreneur's control produces greater partnerships and results. These are perspectives to remember."

~ Christopher Doroh

"Credit for achievement bolsters an entrepreneur's perception of their business and the control they have for creating value. This can be a very valuable tool for positively influencing entrepreneurs. If an entrepreneur perceives that credit due them was given to a support person instead, their perception of control will diminish, along with their relationship with those presenting the achievement and those who received the "undue" credit."

~ Dr. Bernard Franklin

"The reason entrepreneurs need to perceive control is that they are making business changes to gain future financial opportunities. The common mistake is having experienced coaches directing the business toward current opportunities when the entrepreneur is focused on the future."

~ Michie P. Slaughter

result…entrepreneurs get all of the credit in their own minds and from the center, which will empower entrepreneurs to come back the next time they become stuck.

Credit for new discoveries or business accomplishments should flow from the community, government and civic leaders directly back to the entrepreneur, and not initially be credited to a mentor, coach or some other outside source. If one takes away that sense of accomplishment, the entrepreneur will perceive a lack of control and will reject even the best insights and discoveries that are helping his/her business. But when the entrepreneur receives the credit and experiences the accomplishment, this will then drive him/her to the next great discovery.

The perceived control of free will is a significant mindset that drives entrepreneurs to reach outcomes and goals. This mindset should also help provide some clarity for government and civic leaders as to why entrepreneurs act so erratically in certain environments or in certain situations.

The Perceived Control of Free Will Mindset

Mindset 5: Needs vs. Wants Paradigm

"Our necessities never equal our wants."
~ Benjamin Franklin

Entrepreneurs have continual **needs** and **wants** during business startup and growth phases. Examples of these constant **needs** are money, investors, and promotions. Examples of constant **wants** are customers, mentoring, marketing and sales, guidance, training and coaching. (At this point it may seem as though the examples for needs and wants were switched accidentally, but in fact entrepreneurs often perceive them in this fashion.) Needs are top-of-mind; wants are often out-of-mind. So the wants and needs listed above are actually reversed, since the 'nice to have' wants in these examples are essential for any business to succeed.

The need for money, investors, and promotions by entrepreneurs causes program vendors, mentors, coaches, and anyone else trying to support startups and growing businesses, a lot of frustration. This is because the solutions they offer to entrepreneurs (customers, mentoring, marketing and sales, guidance and training, and coaching) are

"Entrepreneurs are often given anything but a clear direction to start or grow their businesses. So the assets that are often sought out are universally valuable. These universally valuable "needs" are investment, promotion, and money. These needs are valuable, but to maximize their value entrepreneurs must FIRST have a strategy and clear direction. To gain this direction requires "wants" that are less regularly sought out."

~ Barry J Crocker

perceived as "nice to have" wants and are not in high demand.

For example, Josh Leonard, an investment capital expert, FBI Agent, and current entrepreneur, regularly meets with Kansas City entrepreneurs to advise them on starting or growing their businesses. Josh admits that his advice is often dismissed as entrepreneurs see it as a solution to a lesser problem...a want. A specific example of this is when entrepreneurs seek capital and dismiss advice for how to first seize revenue opportunities. Entrepreneurs are almost always better off finding customers prior to investors. Market validation of business assumptions is one of the common critical criteria in determining business valuation and investor equity stakes. The lure of investor capital as a solution for growth prior to sales prematurely draws many business owners toward the perceived big win of an investor. Josh recognizes that while changing the entrepreneur's perspective he must also keep their perception of free will intact to continue working with him, so he tries to reason with them as to how sales can generate enough revenue to meet their financial needs. However, Josh says that while many see the real revenue opportunities, many more will continue to focus on a single big win. Josh doesn't agree with all their decisions, however, he respects that it is their business and their decision to make.

Michie Slaughter, formerly the Founding President of the Kauffman Foundation's Center for Entrepreneurial Leadership, suggests that an effective way to support entrepreneurs is to use their perceived needs as a "carrot" to focus them on the development of the wants that will effectively start and build their business. For example, entrepreneurs can be offered an introduction to an investor or an opportunity to present at an entrepreneurial event if they first achieve set milestones in building their business. While this may seem counter to their perception of control, in reality the entrepreneur has the option to engage and knows that by achieving set milestones he/she will gain access to a perceived need.

"Entrepreneurs often, not always, misunderstand what their business needs are versus what sounds appealing. This relates to the context gap and lack of experiences. The quick fix is leveraging the proverbial carrot of wants to attract entrepreneurs to address their needs first."

~ Danny Lobina

This carrot approach can help support program vendors, mentors, coaches, and resource services understand how they can increase the appeal of their offerings - the entrepreneurs' wants - by appealing to the business owners' heavily sought after needs. The needs vs. wants paradigm also explains a lot about entrepreneurs seemingly chaotic actions and decision-making, and provides an understanding for how to channel this mindset for the betterment of both the support community and entrepreneur's business.

The Needs vs. Wants Paradigm Mindset:

Entrepreneur Social Infrastructure Review

The purpose of the five mindsets in the Entrepreneur Social Infrastructure is to provide greater understanding for how entrepreneurs think and make decisions in order to make sense of their actions. Government and civic leaders can use these insights to attract and engage entrepreneurs to the community and its support programs. Understanding these mindsets helps leaders envision a better entrepreneur environment for startups or growing businesses. The specific strategies and operations for creating this environment will be discussed in detail in Chapter 8: The Entrepreneur Operational Infrastructure.

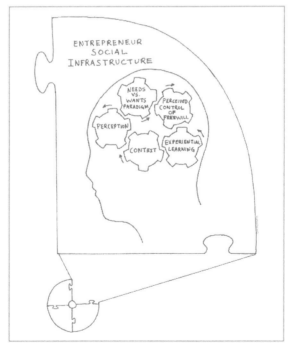

The Entrepreneur Social Infrastructure:
5 mindsets that drive the entrepreneur's thoughts and actions

Now that entrepreneurs are better understood, there is an army of volunteers just waiting to be engaged - the community of people in your city or region. Learning how to amass and be a servant-leader to this army will be essential for achieving a growing and sustainable entrepreneur environment and economy. The volunteer army's effectiveness in helping entrepreneurs will be dependent on utilizing the five entrepreneurial mindsets learned in this Entrepreneur Social Infrastructure.

> *"People will support what is best for the "greater good". Success demands an understanding of how the community thinks and what drives its behaviors. When core behaviors include a desire to grow the community and create a better quality of life for all, entrepreneurship is engaged and an ecosystem is created that provides support at every stage."*
>
> ~ *Corey J. Mehaffy*

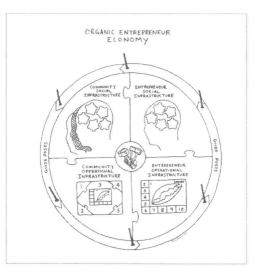

The complete *Organic Entrepreneur Economy*:
Organic Environment, four Infrastructures and 6 Guideposts

Chapter 6:

The Community Social Infrastructure

As excitement for entrepreneurship grew, the Kansas City community began to splinter back into smaller, niche pods with varying degrees of knowledge and support for entrepreneurship. We realized that the less a pod knew about entrepreneurship in their city or region, the less supportive they would be for these business owners. Moreover, community support did not just mean being positive to those already starting or growing a business, but began as the encouragement of friends, family, and others to become or avoid entrepreneurship in the first place. Achieving a well-informed and collaborative pod was necessary to sustain and build a supportive community and culture in Kansas City. While there were pods in Kansas City that were very informed and supportive of entrepreneurship, they remained isolated from influencing the rest of the community. This led to the realization that fostering a supportive community and changing the culture was key to transforming the city and region to become entrepreneurial, in the short-term and long-term.

In Kansas City there were many who agreed with the need to inform and grow support in the community, its culture, and thereby entrepreneurship. One of these people was Jeff Danley, a serial entrepreneur who started Freestyle Media, which provides content to mobile devices. Jeff understood the lack of community support from his own personal experience, and recognized that changing the culture would increase the saturation and growth of entrepreneurs throughout the city and region. Another supportive entrepreneur was Mike Millay, an insurance agency owner from a suburb of Kansas City. Mike's reason for wanting to grow the entrepreneur community was a personal mission to eliminate "paycheck-based loan" stores by creating higher paid jobs that eliminated the need for short-term, high interest rate cash loans. There were many other supportive entrepreneurs, corporations, and individuals who had their reasons for wanting to grow their community, the culture, and the economy. An understanding of Kansas City's community and their mindsets was critical to changing how people thought, made decisions, and acted to support entrepreneurship.

> "GrowBlueSprings, an Organic Environment, provides a continuum of learning for entrepreneurs and engagement roles for local mentors and business coaches. It also positions the Blue Springs community to feel like a supportive family for their businesses, offering entrepreneurs a strong sense of support and opportunity in the Blue Springs community."
>
> ~ Brien M. Starner

Changing an entire community would not be an easy task. How were we going to figure out how a community could support every entrepreneur? That question led to the realization that the primary influencers of any entrepreneur were their family, their friends, and the community around them. These influencers become the entrepreneur's biggest fans and supporters, cheering them on to success. While these influencers in Kansas City were primarily segmented into smaller pods, it showed that there were at least some existing supportive networks assisting entrepreneurs. If we could use the pre-existing pods as a template for how a community could be supportive, perhaps it could be replicated throughout the city and region. To have any chance to motivate and engage the community, we knew it was essential to figure out how these pods of people thought, made decisions, and ultimately supported entrepreneurs.

"A community must create an open and accessible environment, unhindered by over regulation. By doing so, communities create a perception of freedom and compel entrepreneurs to become involved."

~ Dr. Bernard Franklin

The answer was actually fairly straightforward. A community inherently chooses, often unknowingly, whether or not to support entrepreneurship based on the opinions, actions, and perspectives of other people in the community. Essentially, the community was constantly influencing itself toward or away from supporting entrepreneurship.

This led to the identification of the five mindsets that influenced how a community embraced or neglected entrepreneurship:

1. Perception

2. Community Audiences

3. Community Involvement & Empowerment

"Government, civic, and community leaders need to decide how they want their community to think and be motivated in the future if they are to prepare for the entrepreneurial and economic trends of the next 5-7 years."

~Michie P. Slaughter

4. Community Ownership & Free Will

5. Failure Response

To put this into perspective, changing the culture of a corporation is rather straightforward and usually only takes a few years, just as employees are incentivized to change because their paycheck is likely on the line. On the other hand, changing the culture of a community is thought to take 20-30 years and is the natural and slow process for an evolving entrepreneur environment. To organically accelerate this process, one must understand the five community mindsets. An understanding of the mindsets, we realized, can result in orchestrating change much more quickly.

"This cannot be overstated: the Organic Environment binds the Community together. However, that is not the starting point—but rather the ending point. It takes a well-orchestrated strategy to get to that end."

~ Matthew Hart

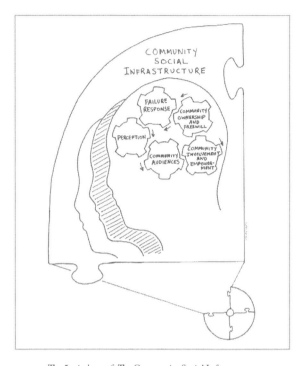

The 5 mindsets of The Community Social Infrastructure

Mindset 1: Perception

"Most of the mistakes in thinking are inadequacies of perception rather than mistakes of logic" ~ Edward de Bono

Perception is the single most powerful force that guides the thoughts, decisions, and actions of a community. Although made up of many individuals, the community is often perceived, by outsiders, to have a singular perspective or culture. The community's perception dictates how that group of people perceive their internal and external environment.

For example, 5-years ago the technology and startup communities were re-establishing a foothold in Kansas City. Many in the suburbs were still unaware of these startups, so we decided to host a new event called PitchON! This event would allow entrepreneurs to pitch their business to investors in front of an attending audience. It was held during one of the first Entrepreneur Week's that Kauffman Foundation created to celebrate entrepreneurship across the world, and was physically held in an Administration Building in Olathe, a suburb of Kansas City. I remember how surprised people were that investors were attending, and many thought they had come from outside the city. During the presentations we had to constantly ask the audience to quiet down because people were getting so excited about the tech startups they never imagined

"The perception of the community is a silent but powerful force. This force can be very beneficial or extremely destructive within a community, though it is rarely controlled. This community mindset is critical to understanding and fostering entrepreneurship and a supportive culture across a city or region."

~ Mark W. Dickey

were in Kansas City. In fact, one woman come up to me afterwards and commented that she could not believe how strong these startup businesses were...for she always thought startups had out of this world dreams that could never be realized. This proved the Advisory Experts and me that just because entrepreneurship is alive and well in a city or region, it does not mean that the community will be supportive of it.

People who do not come into direct contact with or become informed about entrepreneurs and their progress perceive the results based on hearsay and speculation. This was true for the people and woman in the example above. Therefore, understanding the community's perceptions and how they are made is crucial to determining how to position a community to be supportive of entrepreneurs and maintain that positioning.

Perception is the base mindset for the Community Social Infrastructure, as the remaining four mindsets will build upon it. Additionally it is important to understand that the community's perception is constantly evolving and these perception changes are constantly reshaping the culture and the extent of success entrepreneurship can have in that city or region. This evolution occurs as the people, who comprise a community, are constantly influencing each other through interactions and shared perspectives. Thus it is critical to track

"There is no doubt that communities are constantly evolving and changing. This causes the perceptions of people within those communities to change exponentially faster, which makes it very difficult to evaluate the needs and desires of a city or region. Social media only accelerates this. Understanding the community at any one time is challenging, but doing it perpetually is seemingly impossible without a mechanism for deciphering the noise!"

~ Jeff Kaczmarek

the community's perceptions to identify the level of support for or against entrepreneurship.

To help, here is a simple guide for understanding community perceptions:

1. Perceptions are manifested from information that is either provided to or, in the absence of relevant information, speculated by the community.

2. A perception is unique to each person, and when people share their thoughts the resulting perception, known as culture, is unique to the community.

3. Perceptions define fact and fiction for the community, regardless of truth.

4. Community/cultural perceptions guide people's actions and thoughts.

5. These community thoughts and actions will dictate whether or not entrepreneurs are supported in the city or region.

Perceptions act as a "subconscious brain" that guides the community's decision of whether or not to support entrepreneurship.

The communication platforms most likely to influence the communi-

"A Community's perceptions will be largely based on the Comfluencers' and Media's messaging. So it is important to first recognize that this is happening. Then, seek to put a system in place to actively monitor and influence the ever evolving communal perceptions that are guiding the actions in a city or region."

~ Corey J. Mehaffy

ty's perception are the traditional and social media outlets. This occurs because the majority of a community will not actually interact with entrepreneurs but will rather gain information from what they hear, read, or see in the media concerning the entrepreneur environment in their city or region. For example, people who learn about mass riots in a foreign nation via a televised broadcast may have never researched or been to that nation and thus perceive the entire country to be in riots. They may even warn others about the country's riots and discourage travel to that country. If this seems similar to a rumor, it is because perception based on speculation is exactly that. So now you see that a community's perceptions are heavily influenced by traditional and social medias, as well as the power it can have on supporting or working against entrepreneurship.

Two elements that can change any community's perception are safety and benefits. Both of these perception elements are weighed heavily when changing a person's or community's perception. Thus the keys to these elements are:

Safety: The more that is known about entrepreneurs in a city or region, the greater their safety rating. The unknown is often scary and creates a sense of fear, which causes uncontrolled speculation in the community and culture. Also, the phrase "safety in numbers" applies here. The more people in a community who become involved, the safer they consider en-

"Safe and Beneficial are the proverbial 'Swiss Army Knives' of evaluating and attracting community support. The success of grassroots or political efforts can be predicted based upon their safety and benefits! These are strong influencers when working to change a culture in support of entrepreneurship."

~ Mark W. Dickey

trepreneurship. Thus people are open to engaging in actions and decisions that are considered safe, a positive perception.

Benefits: Individuals in a community must perceive benefits from entrepreneurship before they will consider offering support or participation. These benefits can be the growth in jobs, a better quality of life, or some perceived benefit more specific to the community. What is important is that the community can identify strong outcomes in supporting entrepreneurship, as this will encourage discussion and advocacy. People enjoy making decisions or taking actions that are beneficial, and so this appeals to a positive perception.

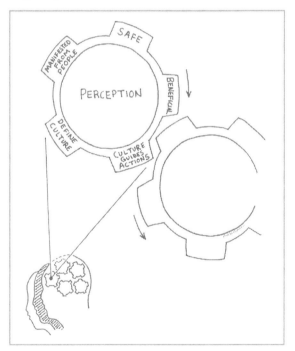

The Perception Mindset

For example, think hypothetically about investing your money in a startup or in a bank. Both options immediately bring to light some perceptions from your past experiences. For some the bank is clearly both the most safe and provides the most beneficial, though minimal, 1 return, though minimal. Others may select angel investors, and perceive the right startup to be both safe and very beneficial. Regardless of your preference, this points to the fact that people perceive options to be either positive or negative, based on their perception of safety and benefit. Gaining a cultural shift in support for entrepreneurship relies on the community perceiving business creation and growth to be safe and beneficial.

To establish a positive community perception of entrepreneurship, they must perceive safety and benefits in four additional mindsets:

- Community Audiences

- Community Involvement and Empowerment

- Community Ownership and Free Will

- Failure Response

These mindsets will offer further insights into how and why a community of people think, make decisions, and act as they do to help government and civic leaders better understand the culture and how to gain support and involvement from the community to foster entrepreneurship in their city or region. The next mindset explores the Community Audiences and their roles in influencing and mobilizing the community.

Mindset 2: Community Audiences

"Communication leads to community, that is, to understanding, intimacy and mutual understanding."
~ Rollo May

In a community, people are the mechanism of stability, change, and action. However, not everyone's role in this mechanism is equal, as some categories of people are much more influential or involved than others. Changing a culture and position the community to support entrepreneurship requires an understanding of the importance of each category, how they are motivated, and how they effectively influence others in the community.

The three main **Community Audiences** are:

1. *Highly Motivated People* (or **Doers**) – These people are highly productive, organized, and motivated to work for themselves and the benefit of the community. They are often entrepreneurs, high-achieving young professionals, and vice presidents of small and medium-sized businesses, as well as administrative assistants who work to build initiatives. Doers are motivated by praise from the community and outcomes of the initiatives, as well as personal financial rewards.

2. *Community Influencers* (or **Comfluencers**) – These people are highly networked and connected within the community, as they were often Doers earlier in life. Their opinions are valued, have a strong influence on community perceptions, and can often motivate others to take action. They are typically motivated by gaining greater influence, praise, recognition, access to impor-

tant connections, and building the prosperity of their community. Often these people are mature and experienced executives, repeatedly successful as entrepreneurs, presidents of small or medium-sized businesses, vice presidents at larger corporations, politicians, or government and civic leaders. *(Presidents and chief executive officers of large, national or international corporations are typically not Comfluencers in a city or region, but rather on a national stage. For while they are respected in their own operations and known externally, they are often focused on a national or global community.)*

3. *Community-at-Large* (or **CAL**) – The majority of people in a community comprise a CAL. While the CAL seldom acts, it typically does so as a unit and is able to provide swift change to the culture and actions in the community. Unfortunately, a CAL is easily divided and distracted, and so getting action from this unit often requires the unified support of many of the Comfluencers and Doers. The people within the CAL are motivated by the betterment of the community and incentives provided to all. The CAL category is essentially composed of everyone that is not a Doer or Comfluencer.

Segmenting the audiences into these three categories allows for an understanding of how to effectively and efficiently influence the community to support entrepreneurship in

"Grouping people into categories is difficult and fluctuates based on the application. In this context, the break down is helpful for understanding how a community works, so each audience can be effectively motivated to embrace and support entrepreneurs in their city or region."

~ Lisa Franklin

the city or region. For this reason it is critical to understand how the three community segments (Doers, Comfluencers, and CAL) are motivated and engaged to influence community support. As well as to identify what actions may cause these segments to disengage. The next two mindsets, 1) Community Involvement and Empowerment, and 2) Community Owner-ship and Free Will, clarify how to empower and gain involve-ment from the community.

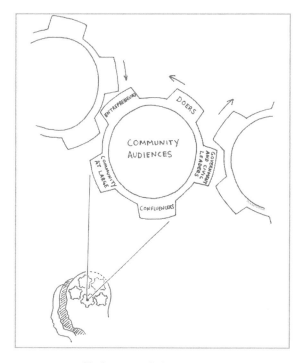

The Community Audiences Mindset

Mindset 3: Community Involvement & Empowerment

"As we look ahead in the next century, leaders will be those who empower others." ~ Bill Gates

Community involvement is a necessity for fostering entrepreneurship. Although many government and civic leaders I have spoken to are attracted to entrepreneurial initiatives, they are concerned by how much time and financial resources the initiatives will take. Community involvement is the only way to achieve a large comprehensive initiative. That said, it is crucial to understand why people in a community become involved in an initiative and how they are empowered to stay involved in order to offset the resources needed.

The primary reasons people in a community get involved in an initiative are the same for an entrepreneur starting a business, either they are passionate or they see an opportunity. In both cases, people are often seeking an active opportunity to be involved. The traditional opportunities for CAL's are either volunteering on the front lines or

"In many communities it is rare to see entrepreneurs, government and civic leaders collaborating to foster community support for entrepreneurs. Communities that actively include entrepreneurs at the government and civic "table" have a much higher success rate in creating a community that fosters and supports entrepreneurial growth."

~ Jo Anne Gabbert

"There is no place for 'command and control' management in the Organic Environment. Great management comes from creating a vibrant environment and then knowing when to slowly,.. back,...away."

~ Matthew Hart

sitting on a board or committee. However, if government and civic leaders want to actually decrease their resource cost, a new opportunity needs to be designed.

In the startup networking group Entrepreneur Roundtable, which hosts monthly breakfasts for 20 and 30-something entrepreneurs, there are scores of people volunteering their time to make each meeting and the group successful. These people are entrepreneurs themselves, and while there is a board in the traditional sense, each seat has a set responsibility to the group. One board member is responsible for recruiting monthly guests to speak at the breakfast, another is responsible for promoting the breakfast, and so on. The awesome insight here is that each board member not only volunteered, but also had to work to get their volunteer position. Thus each board member has a "coordinator" position that brings them in at the top level of decision-making and allows them to be involved in making the group successful.

This same thing happens at startup businesses, where people volunteer their time or work for small portions of equity to be involved at the core. To truly gain involvement that can offset the resources needed it is important to identify how to gain coordinator-level involvement from the commu-

> "The community's involvement is channeled through the coordinators, as these people will ultimately be responsible for elevating their city or region's economy and fostering entrepreneurship. While motivating coordinators was initially a concern of mine, the Organic Environment positions the role in a way that is mutually beneficial for the community and for the person charged with it! Plus, empowering the community to foster their own change always attract involvement."
>
> ~ Lisa Franklin

nity. If you flip back to the descriptions of the Doers and Comfluencers in the last mindset, you will be able to identify how to
attract these two audiences to become involved at a coordinator
level.

The keys to attracting a coordinator tiered volunteer in the
community is:

Sync Community and Professional Benefits - For
example, position a volunteer opportunity as a role that
provides philanthropic benefit to the community AND
professional opportunities. *(Positioning the dual benefits
will ensure the person stays involved even if there is difficulty in their profession or business.)*

Allow for Immediate Involvement - For example,
showcasing a "proposed initiative" to allow the person
to immediately get involved through suggestions.

Make it Epic - Doers and Comfluencers are always
busy, but want to be involved in the next best thing...so
be sure the initiative appeals to their ego.

Show Momentum - Doers and Comfluencers are busy,
but an initiative that seems to already have government
and civic support and is now looking for community
backing will resemble a train that is ready to leave the
station.

Give Space - Those interested in volunteering will likely
have different styles that may not always jive...so be sure
to provide a framework that allows these individuals to

identify how they can best accomplish their tasks.

Community-led - It is important for people who volunteer in this capacity to believe that they will determine the success as much as the government and civic leaders that are providing oversight. Let them know that it is up to them, and the government and civic leaders won't take over. If government and civic leaders intervene, micromanage or override any decision or activity, volunteers may immediately disengage. Instead, government and civic leaders need to use influence to guide and direct these volunteers.

> *"The involvement of community thought leaders and the action-oriented Doers is essential to influence engagement among the majority of people in a community. In the past, initiatives were announced in a decree fashion, which limited the magnitude of success that was possible when the community truly owned the initiative."*
>
> *~ Dr. Bernard Franklin*

There should be ample opportunities for the CAL to volunteer in smaller capacities. Overlooking the participation of the community's audiences is a big mistake, as these audiences can significantly accelerate the growth and adoption of any entrepreneur initiative, since they are the target market.

Coordinator-tiered volunteerism seems logical in theory, but tough to put into practice. Many government and civic organizations are currently struggling to obtain enough volunteers to fill their existing boards. Offering another community volunteer opportunity would seem to drain the already diminishing pool of volunteers. In Kansas City, those interested in coordinator-tiered volunteer positions were not interested in the traditional board or committee positions. This most likely occurred because a coordinator position makes the volunteer a part of the action, and success is dependent, in-part, on their roles and responsibilities. People who are Doers and Comfluencers prefer this type of role and also live for the opportunity to conquer the unknown or change the community for the better. Plus, Doers and Comfluencers are largely driven by their ego, in a good way. They perceive themselves to be successful, which means they will fiercely work to make the initiative a success...as their self-image is dependent on it. This should provide government and civic leaders with some comfort and clarity as to why these types of volunteers get involved.

Now that we understand how to involve people in the community as coordinators, specifically the Doers and Comfluencers, it is time to identify how to empower them to stay engaged. The keys to empowering a volunteer coordinator are:

"Community involvement that supports and connects entrepreneurs in starting or growing businesses is a rarity for any city or region but results in a thriving economy and culture. In naturally-evolving ecosystems, like Silicon Valley, people in the community have informal roles that evolved over decades. To accelerate these results organically requires semi-structured community coordinators which guide and gain support for entrepreneurs. This community coordination truly heightens a city or region's economic growth potential!"

~ Barry J Crocker

Offer the power needed to make decisions and affect the desired change. As long as expectations are set upfront, volunteers will not abuse or misuse their powers.

Promote developments and celebrate successes as they happen. Be sure that the volunteers get as much, if not more, credit than government and civic leaders.

Regularly ask for insights and offer praise. Asking for insights will make the volunteers feel like they are the select few "trusted advisors," and the praise can provide them boosts of excitement along the way.

Speak to volunteers as equals. Often volunteers are managed. In this case it is important for government and civic leaders to address and speak to these volunteers as equals or peers.

To foster entrepreneurship, government and civic leaders must realize what role the community is playing in achieving success. To reach this goal, leaders must partner with highly influential people in the community who are willing to volunteer to attract greater community participation. This additional attraction will help the community perceive ownership in making their city's or region's economy better through their support of entrepreneurship.

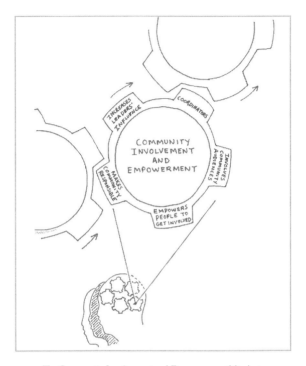

The Community Involvement and Empowerment Mindset

Mindset 4: Community Ownership & Free Will

"When people lack jobs, opportunity, and ownership...they have little or no stake in their communities." ~ Jack Kemp

For the Organic Environment to be able to compel people to support entrepreneurship and truly believe they can grow their economy, they must perceive they have the power to make it succeed or fail. This is important, as Kansas City's Economic Development Corporation did not have the resources or manpower to be able pull off such a large initiative on its own. So it really IS in the community's control. Further, this mindset is the key to any grassroots effort, and can provide government and civic leaders with the insights necessary to influence the outcomes without having to take on the burden of control."

~ Jeff Kaczmarek

Now that the importance of perceptions, involvement, and empowerment have been reviewed for a community and its audiences, we must understand how the role of perceived ownership and free will plays into a community's decision of whether or not to support entrepreneurship.

For a community and its audiences to become engaged and "own" the initiative, they must perceive that their actions and opinions matter in supporting and shaping their culture for entrepreneurship. The community is not seeking ownership for political power or financial gain, but instead they are proud of their city or region and want to be a part of making it better. Think about the small town high school that always regularly competes for state football championships. People in the community support the strong football environment and own the culture by spreading the word about its wins to others. The ownership people seek is recognition from outsiders that they are part of the best football community in the state, and recognition from inside the community for their participation in supporting the football program. Keeping these people in the football community engaged means regularly communicating what is happening so they feel like owners of the information when telling it to others. Individuals and audiences gain a similar feeling of ownership when government and civic leaders communicate information regularly to the community.

Similar to the football analogy, government and civic leaders and their Community Audiences, *which includes coordinators,* must undertake three actions for the ownership of entrepreneurship to occur:

1. Regular communications regarding entrepreneurship in a city or region must be provided to the community.

2. A plan of action must be formulated with defined roles that people in the community can identify with and get behind.

3. A motivated CAL must engage and promote news to people outside the community.

"Influencing the community to emotionally take ownership is a rarity in corporations, and even more rare in city or regional communities. However, the results are astonishing for what can be accomplished when that ownership is strongly embraced. This ownership will strengthen the resolve of the community and bind them together in supporting entrepreneurship and growing the economy."

~ Dr. Bernard Franklin

Some in the community may not support entrepreneurship at first. However, the influence and actions of the Doers and Comfluencers should quickly gain that support. Early supporters will also passionately interact with the rest of the community, which will generate more support.

To achieve ownership and free will, the community must perceive choices in how to support entrepreneurs and their culture. Whether this is offered through a survey or is allowed to organically occur, government and civic leaders should celebrate how the community has decided to support entrepreneurs through their culture. This will further reinforce the community's perception of free will.

Early on in our development of StartKC, the first prototype of the Organic Environment utilizing the infrastructures, we had a meeting with many of the contributing entrepreneurs, business executives, and government and civic leaders to discuss what type of entrepreneurs to focus on. This started a 90-minute discussion that ended where it started...everyone was unsure. So I suggested that we initially use a broad focus until we determined which entrepreneurs would engage. I left the suggestion open-ended with, "What do you think?" The group discussed it for five more minutes and then agreed that a broad focus should be taken. We thanked them for their insight and agreed it was a great idea. Interestingly they perceived the agreement to have been their own and left the meeting excited about the decision to focus on entrepreneurship in a general sense. These supporters perceived ownership and free will in making that decision and in return gave us permission to make future decisions without them. This may seem like an irrelevant meeting, however, these supporters volunteered significant time and financial resources over the next several years, regularly mentioning how awesome it was for them to decide which direction we focused on!

Government and civic leaders may feel they are handing over perceived ownership and control to the community, they are actually gaining influence over a community that is quickly becoming passionate for entrepreneurship. This influence is actually a stronger and more persuasive version of control than status or title, and is the most efficient way to mobilize the community toward economic outcomes.

"Free will is the mechanism that defines whether ownership is an illusion or reality. It is critical that people in a community, especially those with influence, perceive free will to influence and grow the initiative. Otherwise they will feel duped, perceiving that ownership is in name only. Free will is essential when motivating a community."

~ Dr. Bernard Franklin

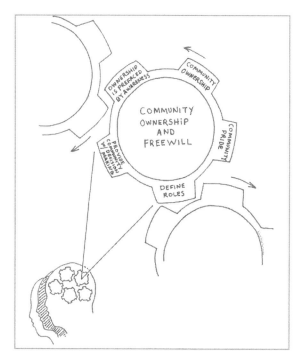

The Community Ownership and Free Will Mindset

Mindset 5: Failure Response

"The fear of failure is simply a gut reaction to an immeasurable risk" – unknown

One of the most powerful, and potentially destructive, forces in changing a community culture to support entrepreneurship is the "fear of" and the "response to failure". In fact, it's not even how a community responds, but rather how entrepreneurs perceive they will respond. This perceived response is often the greatest determiner for why an entrepreneur decides not to start a business. Every entrepreneur, whether trying to raise investment capital, talking to new potential customers, or pitching a concept to an aggressive CEO thinks about what could happen if they fail. So it is of utmost importance for a community and culture to identify their perception of failure and how people are likely to respond.

The key to achieving this culture is to have influential and successful people talk about their failures and tell how those negative experiences have actually helped them to achieve success in the future. The focus here is to generate awareness of a largely unknown, and often taboo, event known as business failure and how this experience is often a part of the learning process for achieving entrepreneurial success. This will encourage entrepreneurs to see that while failing is unpleasant, the community is still supportive and willing to help them achieve success. Bankruptcy is in fact a method to manage and control failures that allows for subsequent success.

When the fear of failure is understood entrepreneurs are likely to seek help early and often, instead of waiting until their businesses are on the brink of failure. Entrepreneurs are not known for standing up in a public place to declare they are failing and need help! Instead, they instinctively disengage from their involvements and keep frustration inside. Their reluctance to ask for help causes unnecessary business failures that could have been avoided. Communities simply cannot afford to have these unnecessary failures and the resulting losses in jobs, economic outputs, and tax base. The exploration of failures and making the perceived failure response more collaborative and supportive, would enable entrepreneurs to communicate their issues earlier on, significantly reducing their chances of failing. The Small Business Administration reports that nearly half of all small businesses fail in the first 5 years; while franchise businesses, those with a strong support network, have an estimated 95% chance of success during the same period.

> *"Failure is the best learning experience. Failing early and often prevents catastrophic failures down the road. It is imperative to understand failure and its beneficial outcomes, as overcoming failure is a critical aspect in growing a community, entrepreneurial business, and the economy!"*
>
> ~ Mark W. Dickey

To put this into context, the Evis Consulting team and I are all entrepreneurs, and are constantly hitting small failures in the form of the word "NO" when testing pitches for new concepts. Collectively we expect to fail 50% of the time, and if we don't fail at that rate we are not marketing to new customers very aggressively. Understanding where customer and market needs aren't is the fastest way to identify where the best opportunities actually are. Failure response inside our company is supportive and celebrates small failures as necessary to avoid larger ones in the future. Each entrepreneur at Evis Consulting has failed at least once, yet together we are successful today thanks to the lessons collectively learned.

In reality, fear of failure is an entrepreneur's gut response to an immeasurable risk. So risk and making smart decisions play a big role in the fear of failure. When risks are understood, failure is put into context and is less scary and less of a detractor. Entrepreneurs are constantly struggling with measuring risks in this way, as this metric guides their perceptions, decision-making, and ultimately their actions.

When a promising start-up business fails, communities rarely communicate the circumstances, and thus people's perception of entrepreneurship as being safe and beneficial begins to fade. So it is of paramount importance for a community to realize how their failure response affects their culture and entrepreneur environment, and to always communicate developments, whether good or bad.

"Government and civic organizers have a two-fold role when it comes to failure response: convincing the community and the civic or government entity (that is investing in the Organic Environment) that failure is part of the entrepreneur's learning curve and stripping away the perceived taboo."

~ *Matthew Hart*

"Entrepreneurs who fail one or multiple times learn at a faster rate than those who don't. Too often communities look at failure as negative and withhold support from entrepreneurs who want to start a new venture. In fact, entrepreneurs who fail are often more successful in future ventures. Communities should recognize that failure happens…even to the best entrepreneurs. In my opinion, failure should be seen as a badge of honor."

~*Jo Anne Gabbert*

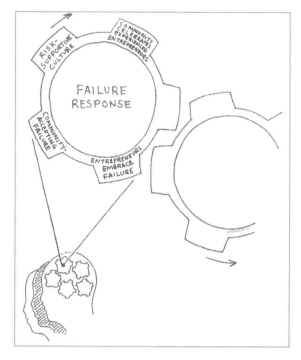

The Failure Response Mindset

Community Social Infrastructure Review

The intricate and complex process to build entrepreneurship and a supportive community can be greatly simplified by understanding how a community and its audiences think, make decisions, and take action. The five mindsets of the Community Social Infrastructure provide these insights and show how the community is a natural fit to achieve change through volunteering. The community and culture are extremely important in achieving exponential economic growth, as they will recruit the entrepreneurs into a city or region and direct them to the support programs they need. While government and civic leaders can lobby and influence for entrepreneur and economic growth, it is the community and its audiences that make the decision and have the power to adapt quick changes and lasting outcomes.

The five mindsets are put into strategic use in the next chapter: Community Operational Infrastructure. The Community Audiences and roles will be operationally organized to support entrepreneurship and grow the economy, assuming government and civic leaders understand how to involve and empower their city or region.

> "The Community Social Infrastructure mindsets are key to understanding how to build a thriving entrepreneur environment and then reshaping the community's perspectives about what's possible regarding entrepreneurs, risks, potential outcomes and networked supporters. These mindsets provide an understanding for how a community's culture is established, as well as how it can be shifted to better support entrepreneurs."
>
> ~ Brien M. Starner

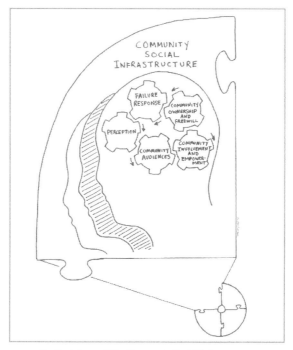

The 5 mindsets of The Community Social Infrastructure

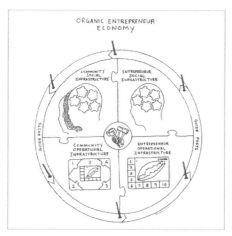

The complete *Organic Entrepreneur Economy*:
Organic Environment, four Infrastructures and 6 Guideposts

Chapter 7:

The Community Operational Infrastructure

Lisa Franklin is a Manager of Economic Development and LocationOne at Kansas City Power & Light (KCP&L). Lisa and KCP&L were early supporters of the Organic Environment and its use by cities and regions, as they too believed that the community was the key to entrepreneurship. Lisa's perspectives were incredibly insightful as she pointed out that entrepreneurship and business-building are led by people. While these people need professional support for their entrepreneurial businesses, they are also being constantly supported through friendships, parents, family, and other social groups that make up their community. So entrepreneurs are actually being supported equally by their community and professional services, thus inherently rooting entrepreneurship in the local and regional networks of people. It was realized that the key to accelerating the formation of a city's or region's business or economic ecosystem was through community awareness and support. The Organic Environment was designed to operationally accelerate the community's adoption and support of entrepreneurship!

The Organic Environment is fueled by entrepreneurs and their businesses, but the ignition and propulsion comes from the community and its motivated audiences. Many entrepreneurial cities or regions are recognized for attracting the best entrepreneurs to their city. Early entrepreneurs starting their businesses were those that lived and worked in the area. As entrepreneurial activity and successes are making headlines in a new city or region, rest assured there is a community engaged and working diligently behind the scenes to support these businesses and help them reach their milestones. Only when a community commits to being involved and supportive, can entrepreneurs gain the access and resources they need to start a business...not to mention early customers.

> "The Social and Operational Infrastructures were the answer I was long awaiting. It first builds a base understanding and metric for the evolving environment and then provides the structure to build upon going forward. Like building a ship, the Organic Environment provides the blueprints to build the ship as well as how to empower the crew to construct and operate the vessel."
>
> ~ Jeff Kaczmarek

To achieve a strong and supportive community that is both heavily involved and fiercely supportive, the Community Social Infrastructure mindsets discussed in the last chapter must be understood and applied. The Community Operational Infrastructure in this chapter depicts how to strategically put those mindsets to use. This ensures that the community is knowledgeable and actively engaged to support the culture and the entrepreneurial activities needed to organically accelerate an economy.

The Community Operational Infrastructure is comprised of the operational strategies and structures to guide government and civic leaders on how to put the community mindsets into motion. It is important to remember that these leaders can provide a support network to orchestrate connections to entrepreneur programs. However, government or civic organizations should not operate these programs, as this should be done by community vendors. *(The operations containing the entrepreneur programs will be discussed in the next chapter: Entrepreneur Operational Infrastructure.)* To clarify this point using a continuation of the football analogy, think about how parents of high school athletes are often asked to volunteer at the snack bar during sporting events and help at various other activities to generate money for their kid's teams. In essence, the parents act as a community that supports and volunteers time for the team's benefit, even though they are not a coach or in charge of managing the sports team. Similarly a community can actively support entrepreneurial businesses from the sidelines by volunteering or offering moral support.

"Building the Operational Infrastructures on top of learned Social Infrastructures is similar to surveying the land before building physical infrastructures. This provides certainty to leaders that their infrastructures are appropriately planned and can be effectively implemented for the intended results."

~ Lisa Franklin

The operational strategies guide government and civic leaders as they engage the community and its audiences in support of entrepreneurship. By first understanding the community and entrepreneurial mindsets, government and civic leaders now have a clear perspective for how their actions will cause engagement and produce results.

The Community Program Infrastructure simplifies the

complex sets of activities required by Community Audiences, predominantly being the Doers and Comfluencers, to support startups and grow businesses, promote the entrepreneurial progress to the CAL, and form a strategic direction that an entire city or region can support. This complex set of activities that affects entrepreneurs is often unknown or overlooked because it is not obvious. Failure to recognize and involve the Community Audiences in these activities can cause frustration, which may lead to unexpected push-back for an otherwise beneficial initiative or program. That said, any community reaction, whether positive or negative, can now be better interpreted through the use of the community mindsets.

Early on, we realized that community support of entrepreneurship could be the answer to accelerating the achievement of the Organic Environment. This was the moment we decided to go all-in. While at the time this decision seemed less pivotal, it was the time when the Evis Consulting team decided to make this the primary focus and my sole focus. The Advisory Experts agreed to provide assistance and guide us along the way. They helped us realize that we did not have a large checkbook nor hundreds of employ-

> *"Community involvement is often assumed to be the masses taking a desired action that has been asked of them, rather than their own involvement which is supporting and operating the initiative. The latter is the key to Silicon Valley and other economies that have an engaged energy that pulses through the entire population. Understanding how to operationally establish this involvement in a grassroots manner produces extraordinary entrepreneurial and economic results."*
>
> *~ Dr. Bernard Franklin*

ees to orchestrate the community and entrepreneur operations inside our company. Instead, they addressed the importance of empowering the community to do most of the work.

Designing a program for community volunteers to invest time and money into was laughed at by many at the time. But this crazy design led to the methodology that would make organically accelerating entrepreneurship and the economy possible. If it weren't for this ill-advised approach, the Organic Environment would never have been realized and *The Organic Entrepreneur Economy* would never have been authored. But it was!

Early momentum in Kansas City was evident by the energy and excitement of the entrepreneurs and by the many audiences in the community. This excitement was apparent the day after a startFEST event. While sitting in a coffee shop, I overheard two people in the community talking about how the entrepreneurs in the previous night's event were a testament to how their city was evolving. I was about to stroke my own ego by gracing these two people with my presence, when one asked who the event was put on by. The other answered that it was community-led, and that was their job to keep it going. To me this was both a humbling and exhilarating moment! It meant that the community was beginning to adopt the culture of support, and Kansas City was starting to mobilize toward greater support of its entrepreneurs. I remember thinking that this could be the start of Kansas City's acceleration towards a vibrant entrepreneurial landscape just like the one in Silicon Valley!

For government and civic leaders to successfully guide a community to become a supportive and fertile entrepreneur environment, it is important to understand the five operations of the Community Operational Infrastructure:

1. Community-Embraced Brand Identity

2. Community-Driven Focuses

3. Community-Led Organic Environment

4. Community-Focused Results

5. Community-Shared Empowerment

"The strength of "community-led" is that it allows creativity and passion to be a focal point. Those who understand "why" this is important will become the leaders. Those who figure out how to apply the "why" will drive change and help the community overcome any challenge that is faced."

~Michie P. Slaughter

Each of the five operations, and accompanying strategies, are specifically targeted to support and enrich specific elements in the Organic Environment by showing the community how to foster a growing economy.

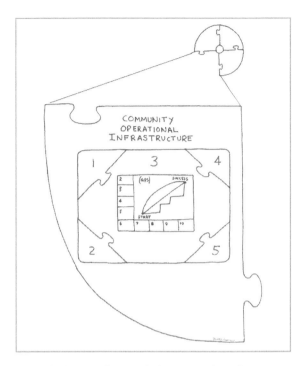

The Community Operational Infrastructure with it's 5 Operations

Operation 1: Community-Embraced Brand Identity

"Your premium brand had better be delivering something special, or its not going to get the business." ~ Warren Buffett

The brand identity of a city or regional Organic Environment serves as a strong and constant reminder to the community and entrepreneurs of how the initiative was formed and what it stands for. This is the first opportunity for government and civic leaders to put the community mindsets into practice as they work with their audiences to create the brand. It is critical to collect community input and then communicate the branding decision in gaining community support from the start. Also, this brand can either conjure up positive or negative thoughts by the community, which will directly correlate to future involvement. So the community must be engaged, embrace and take ownership in the brand creation process of their Organic Environment!

That said, the process for choosing branding need not be long and arduous or involve the entire community. Instead, government and civic leaders should leverage the help of the Community Audiences to identify

"Collective community branding of entrepreneurship is very important. Community branding tells the story of why entrepreneurs are welcome and can succeed in a particular city or region. Quality branding attracts new businesses, a qualified work force, visitors and investors that can foster and grow an entrepreneurial community. Just as professional sports bring bragging rights to a city, so too does economic growth generated by community supported and branded entrepreneurs."

~Jo Anne Gabbert

and choose an action-oriented brand that represents the whole community. These audiences are able to speak for the entire community, as they are part of it, and because they are in tune with the city's or region's wants and needs. During this process, the Doers and Comfluencers will be primarily involved, so it is important for them to promote the branding options to the community-at-large.

For example Corey Mehaffy, co-founder of GrowMidMo's Organic Environment and President of Moberly Area Economic Development Corporation, offers this simplified perspective, "Every community has a story...it just needs to be identified and promoted." Corey's advice simply means that every city or region has desired goals and focus points. The Organic Environment simply provides an avenue to tell the story organically through grassroots efforts and to manifest the desired focus points. Often a city's or region's leaders find themselves struggling with how to reach their desired goals. The Organic Environment is a way to organically produce the promotion and economic outcomes throughout the community. Corey has proven his abilities to help Moberly and the four surrounding counties tell their story and reach their goals by focusing on telling the desired message. The community-led Organic Environment, GrowMidMO, is a part of the strategy that Corey utilizes and helps other cities embrace as well.

For government and civic leaders to facilitate the community-embraced branding in conjunction with the Community Audiences, they must:

1. Choose a Name - The name is best when it is an "action word + name of city or region."

2. Choose a Logo Design - The logo design should include the name and anything else that resonates with the Community Audiences, and also what they believe will resonate with the rest of the community.

3. Personalize the Brand to Appeal to the Community - Personalizing the brand requires Community Audiences to describe what the brand means and what it will accomplish for the community and entrepreneurs. This description must then be promoted to the community, who will then begin perceiving ownership. *(Though the brand of a chamber of commerce, city, county, region, or economic development organization can appear alongside the city's or region's Organic Environment brand, they must remain independent of each other for entrepreneurs and the community to perceive it as a grassroots effort.)*

"Community involvement in the branding of its Organic Environment gives the community a sense of empowerment and ownership. This process is critical to help create a sustainable environment for entrepreneurs."

~ Brien M. Starner

For example, GrowBlueSprings, BoostLeesSummit, and GrowMidMO were some of the branded Organic Environments, which followed the footsteps of Kansas City's StartKC. Each brand was picked by the Community Audiences through a process facilitated by government and civic leaders in those cities or regions. As the Community Audiences worked to choose a brand, they maintained constant communication, obtained perspectives and shared description of the initiative with others in the community. Since the brand was chosen collaboratively, the corresponding community perceived a greater sense of positivity and opportunity from it.

Throughout the strategic branding process it is crucial for government and civic leaders, and those audiences heavily engaged, to remember the five community mindsets. Attracting early and long-term community engagement is critical! Thus each time a person or community audience hears the brand of their Organic Environment, it will instill satisfaction that they are part of the grassroots effort that will result in long-term opportunities.

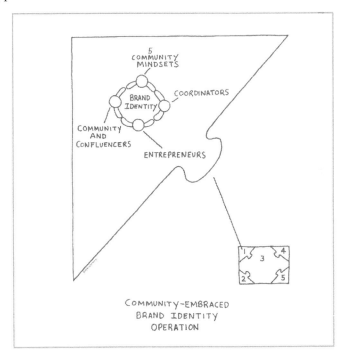

Community-Embraced Brand Identity Operation

Operation 2: Community-Driven Focuses

"Coming together is a beginning; keeping together is progress; working together is success." ~ Henry Ford

The Community-driven focuses set the direction and define the outcomes that a city or regionally branded Organic Environment will work towards accomplishing. The outcomes should have three primary focuses involving industries *(i.e. biotech, tech, manufacturing)* or business types *(i.e. high-growth startup, small business, lifestyle business)*. Focal points can be set for new or existing industries or business types. The benefit of the community-driven focus approach is that new industry clusters and business types can be grown with the aid of community support when utilizing the Community Operational Infrastructure.

The setting of community-driven focuses should be facilitated by Community Audiences and influenced by government and civic leaders, though at times some facilitation may be needed by the leaders to reach a decision. Ultimately, it is important for the CAL to be made aware of the focus options and the decision that has been primarily made by the Community Audiences. The more the community is included in this collaborative process, the greater their sense of ownership, involvement and support. These community-driven focuses can and will influence the direction of the community, entrepreneurship, and the resulting culture.

"Every city or region has a story, but it must be told to achieve economic outcomes. The ability to add purposefully to that story allows the community to choose its own economic future."

~ Corey J. Mehaffy

80% of communications sent to the community regarding the Organic Environment needs to center on the three primary community-driven focuses, with the other 20% may focus on general industries and business types. The amount of communication each focus receives will most likely correlate with the community's amount of perceived activity by entrepreneurs in each focus area. Communications on the progress made in each focal area should be updated as needed.

This is an example of how the four focuses and percentage of communications *(by the Coordinator Teams)* can be positioned:

1. Green Energy Promotion = 20%

2. Aerospace Promotion = 20%

3. High-growth Startups Promotion = 40%

4. General Focus Promotion = 20%

This approach will rapidly change community perceptions of the productivity of their entrepreneurs and businesses. Changing these interactions is extremely powerful, as this quickly changes the culture...voluntarily! These focal points create a perception of strong and purposeful growth in the tar-

"Communication sent out as part of the community-led Organic Environment is incredibly valuable as these messages will initially set the community's expectations and then will help guide those perceptions into the future. Channeling communications toward specific industries will undoubtedly increase the community's perception for greater entrepreneur activity and economic growth in those areas. This communication format increases the influence of government and civic leaders in directing their community's future growth."

~ Barry J Crocker

get industries or businesses. The community will instantly notice the benefits that come from supporting entrepreneurs and become further involved. As such, *The Organic Entrepreneur Economy* can organically accelerate the formation of an entrepreneur ecosystem and economy in just 18-24 short months, as opposed to the lengthy 20 - 30 years that is naturally required!

"Knowing your regions entrepreneurial strengths is an extremely powerful tool for a community. A community that understands what successes are being realized, can begin to use that information to attract other entrepreneurs and investors to their region. Success attracts success and investment. This knowledge can be used to foster growth in a regions entrepreneurial strengths, but all entrepreneurship should be incentivized…even if not in proportion."

~Jo Anne Gabbert

Again, it does not matter whether the three primary focuses are already prevalent in the city or region. After the Community Operational Infrastructure is put in place, communications about the entrepreneurial progresses will increase and the community will perceive a shift in business and economic growth toward these three focal points.

The community-driven focuses operation closely resembles and was modeled after Dr. Bernard Franklin's Imagineering, a process for realizing future potential. Dr. Franklin's process involves recognizing the current status of an environment *(whether an organization, community, or even a workplace)* and identifying future, desired environments to build towards. The community-driven focuses closely follow Dr. Franklin's process to create fast and lasting results through the process of identifying the focuses, crafting a plan to make the focuses a reality, and then working to execute the plan. Dr. Franklin admits the perceptions, views, and beliefs of those involved will either usher in the new results or grind progress to a standstill. The mindsets are also a significant determinant of success for the community-driven focuses.

Thus the community mindsets are crucially important because the four focuses must be driven by the community. Government and civic leaders need to understand how the specific mindsets *(i.e. perception, community ownership, community involvement & empowerment, and Community Audiences)* are utilized to achieve the community-driven focuses, thereby ensuring the community stays engaged and supportive as their economy and environment transform around them.

Community-driven focuses are implemented through direct interaction with the community, as this will create an experience for each person who helps choose the economic direction for their city or region. When people learn more about their industries and entrepreneurs, they experience a sense of ownership that motivates them to get involved and support these focuses. The result is a culture change by supporting entrepreneurs in the chosen industries or business types and realizing that desired economic outcomes are possible and in reach. Thus the community-driven focus operation is a critical step in achieving community involvement to support entrepreneurship.

"Influencing early Focus areas will be a tricky business. Government and Civic leaders can't let themselves be caught up in this step for too long. Make a decision, check the results, and then calibrate."

~ Matthew Hart

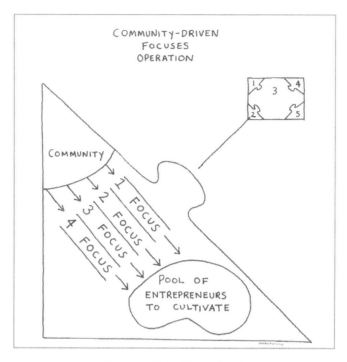

Community-Driven Focuses Operation

Operation 3: Community-Led Organic Environment

"Do you know what my favorite renewable fuel is? An ecosystem for innovation." ~ Thomas Friedman

The community-led organic environment operation is the recruitment of specific Community Audiences - previously referred to as volunteer coordinators - to lead community involvement and achieve desired outcomes. Coordinators take the lead in supporting entrepreneurs by aggregating the resources, experienced professionals, and support programs available in the city or region. This is different, but actually makes perfect sense, as people that have the most insights and best perspectives for how to start and grow businesses are those already living and working in a geographic community. Therefore, having coordinators volunteer from Community Audiences and actively support operations and build connection networks for entrepreneurs makes sense and is economical. This finally provides government and civic leaders with a directive that the community owns and allows for a public-private partnership that is completely in sync!

Doers and Comfluencers take on their operational roles as coordinators, organically recruit other people

"Coordinators are the "ring leaders" for rallying entrepreneurial support from the community. They develop a partnerships with business and community leaders to attract intimate support for entrepreneurship and business owners across the communal masses. Allowing those in the community to be coordinators or "ring leaders" allows for the grassroots nature to be sustained as the economy grows."

~ Mark W. Dickey

from the community to join them, and seek out new or undiscovered entrepreneurs to participate in their branded Organic Environment. Now, it is possible that there may be existing entrepreneur programs and incubators that perceive the branded Organic Environment to be a threat or competitor, rather than a connector of their services to entrepreneurs. So coordinators also become ambassadors to pre-existing entrepreneur support organizations or vendors and help all audiences understand the intent and benefits of the Organic Environment. The coordinators' ambassador role helps ensure that the entire community and all support programs and vendors are informed, dissipating any perceived unknown or fear of competition.

"Identifying key comfluencers in your community to be coordinators is critical. Coordinators bring their own expertise and network to the program. Their ability to attract talent and plug them into the program where their expertise is needed is a key to success."

~ Corey J. Mehaffy

Mark Dickey, the Administrator for Boost Lee's Summit and Vice President of the Lee's Summit Chamber of Commerce, was very instrumental in realizing how coordinators could work in teams to generate support for entrepreneurs. Mark pointed out to the Advisory Experts that these community-focused coordinators had the connections and charisma to reach out to the many Comfluencers and efluencers in the community to appeal for their support. Mark also realized that suggesting change is almost always better received in person from a peer or friend. In fact, Boost Lee's Summit's Organic Environment, with the help of their coordinator teams, have launched dozens of businesses from ideas into success and accelerated the growth of many existing businesses.

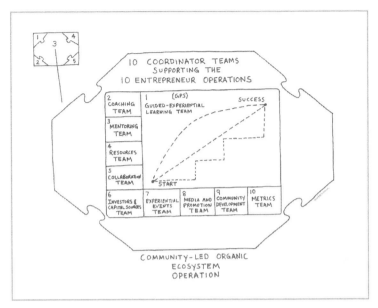

Community-Led Organic Environment:
10 Coordinating Teams support the 10 Entrepreneur Operations

That said, it likely seems backwards, and a bit scary, to assign these powerful coordinator roles to the most action-oriented or influential people in the community, especially as they are volunteers. However, most of these action-oriented Doers and influential Comfluencers are already part of the city's or region's governance or on the boards of high-level civic organizations. They already have access to much of the authority being assigned to them, so not much has changed by having these individuals lead and manage the entrepreneur economy and culture.

Coordinators will be able to expertly promote the formation of the branded Organic Environment to the community and entrepreneurs in ways that government or civic leaders cannot. Plus, they will do it simply to improve their city's or region's economic prosperity and be recognized as one of those who guided the Organic Environment's implementation!

In the community-led organic environment, coordinators work in teams to organize, participate in, and communicate each of 10 entrepreneur operations. These 10 entrepreneur operations are:

1. Guided, Experiential Learning

2. Coaching

3. Mentoring

4. Resources

5. Collaboration

6. Investors and Capital Sources

7. Experiential Events

8. Media and Promotion

9. Community Development

10. Metrics

"A coordinator team allows for individuals to collaborate, combine their networks, and hold each other accountable. A team working toward the same community/entrepreneur goal achieves momentum more quickly than an individual going at it alone."

~ Mark W. Dickey

(Each entrepreneur operation is detailed in the next chapter: Entrepreneur Operational Infrastructure.)

Each coordinator team should consist of three people, who are likely to be Doers or Comfluencers, and is accountable for supporting an entrepreneur operation. Each team is also responsible for organizing support programs and vendors, attracting community involvement, and communicating progress of the entrepreneurs and the Organic Environment to the rest of the community. Coordinator teams organize the operations that generate the support of and participation with entrepreneurs as they work to start and grow businesses in the city or regional Organic Environment.

The description of each entrepreneur operation and the coordinator team's roles and responsibilities are as follows:

1. *Guided, Experiential Learning Operation* - Guides entrepreneurs through startup and business growth processes and teaches skills and insights through situational experiences. Additionally provides training and skills needed through vendors.

Guided, Experiential Learning Team – Focuses on identifying and attracting entrepreneurs from the community to join this program, and match them with business trainers and educators, as well as others who volunteer in *The Organic Entrepreneur Economy*. This team also communicates entrepreneur development to the community and the Media & Promotion Team.

"When you think about the size and scope of energy required, do not be afraid. But do not under-invest in keeping all of these programs connected and calibrated with each other. That's the secret sauce."

~ Matthew Hart

"Guided, Experiential Learning provides "hands-on" accelerated learning in a business outcome format. This key benefit produces successful entrepreneurial ventures in an accelerated timeframe. It is learning by doing!"

~ Brien M. Starner

> "The Coaching operation is critical in attracting those necessary to guide and connect the community's entrepreneurs and help them achieve success. This operation and coordinators helps to support coaches in fostering entrepreneurship and growing the economy."
>
> ~ Danny Lobina

> "Fostering a base of Mentors is essential to accelerating a communities entrepreneurial growth. As Mentors provide entrepreneurs critical experience and insights that they otherwise would not have. Organizing Mentors through the community should be a part of any economic development strategy."
>
> ~ Jo Anne Gabbert

2. *Coaching Operation* - Connects entrepreneurs with business coaches that provide feedback on their businesses, and connect them with contacts such as investors & capital sources, mentoring, resources, and experiential events, among others.

Coaching Team – Asks business coaches and federally funded coaching programs to become part of the Coaching Program, trains coaches on their responsibilities with entrepreneurs in *The Organic Entrepreneur Economy*, and communicates the participating coaches' profiles to the community and Media & Promotion Team.

3. *Mentoring Operation* - Connects startups and existing businesses with successful entrepreneurs who can provide specific guidance and advice in areas where the coach is unable.

Mentoring Team – Recruits successful entrepreneurs from a city or region who are willing to become mentors, and then communicates information about the participating mentors to the community and Media & Promotion Team.

4. Resources Operation - Connects support programs, services, and vendors who provide entrepreneurs the tools and resources needed to startup or grow a business.

Resources Team – Attracts resource and service providers of business-to-business services that support entrepreneurial businesses to join the Resource Operation. They communicate these support programs, services, and vendors to the community and Media & Promotion Team.

5. Collaboration Operation - Gathers entrepreneurs together to share ideas, learn from others' experiences and gain inspiration.

Collaboration Team – Generates opportunities for entrepreneurs to gather with other entrepreneurs and audiences. These collaborative activities, interactions, and experi-

"Resources are valuable, but insights for when to utilize them is even more valuable. As entrepreneurs are often unaware of the problems they have or vendors the need. So assembling the viable resources into an ecosystem is essential, but tricky without the community's and coordinators' involvement. The Resource operations and coordinator team is a MUST for achieving economic growth!"

~ Dr. Bernard Franklin

"Congregating the community and entrepreneurs together to learn and collaborate is pivotal to fostering an entrepreneurial culture and environment. However success is achieved through the structure embedded in the operation and coordinator team, which ensures the collaboration is beneficial and productive."

~ Dr. Bernard Franklin

ences are communicated to the community and Media & Promotion Team.

6. Investors & Capital Sources Operation - Recruits investor and capital sources to join a network of funders, who are connected to screened businesses through business coaches.

> *"Attracting Investors and Capital Sources requires a mechanism to start and grow entrepreneurial businesses and then connect them to the capital. Ironically entrepreneurs are attracted by a large concentration of investors. This operation and coordinator team solves this "chicken or egg" scenario, by building the entrepreneurial mechanism and investor concentration simultaneously. Creating a rich environment for economic growth!"*
>
> *~ Jo Anne Gabbert*

Investors & Capital Sources Team – Finds and recruits angel investors, venture capitalists, banks, and high net-worth individuals to join the Investor & Capital Sources Operation. The number of investors and capital sources that join the network are communicated to the community and any investor or funding source that provides monies to an entrepreneur is communicated to the Media & Promotion Team.

7. Experiential Events Operation - Gives the community opportunity to interact with entrepreneurs they have heard about and provides entrepreneurs an opportunity to refine their pitches, present before investors, and possibly sell to customers. Entrepreneurs earn access to present at the community-hosted events by first completing specified stages of the Guided, Experiential Learning operation and then gaining endorsement from their coaches.

Experiential Events Team – Organizes and promotes the events that showcase entrepreneurs, the support programs, and the coordinator teams. Entrepreneurs that are slated for each event are communicated to the community, and testimonials and success stories from each event are communicated to the Media & Promotion Team. Events also provide the community an opportunity to experience entrepreneurial energy and meet the businesses face-to-face that they have been hearing about through communications.

8. *Media & Promotion Operation* - Promotes the activity of entrepreneurs and those they interact with in their particular city or region to the community and media outlets. The purpose is to gain greater support from the community and to create a more entrepreneurial Organic Environment and culture.

Media & Promotion Team – Collects communications from the other coordinator teams, and then

"Events are incredibly valuable to entrepreneurs and the community as they communicate economic activity through an experience. For the community coordinators this provides awareness for their efforts and validation for the growth that their event-focused efforts are achieving within a region. Having experiential events built for the community, by the community, is an extremely powerful force in enacting economic growth."

~ Barry J Crocker

"Community support is largely a result of an initiative being perceived as "safe" and "beneficial." Mass communication is the most effective influencer of the community's perceptions. Thus the Media & Promotion operation provides the framework for the community's coordinators to foster the desired perception and gain support for the Organic Environment."

~ Barry J Crocker

distributes the information according to the percentages of the community-driven focuses. This team also attracts the attention of mainstream media outlets in the area and uses social media to gain greater community and entrepreneur participation and awareness.

"Community Development channels facts and influences the perception of benefits to reflect a single voice, which will define the community's reality and culture. Coordinators play a pivotal role in reaching that end!"

~ Corey J. Mehaffy

9. Community Development Operation - Aides the other coordinator teams and support programs by engaging with the community to attract specific, additional needs required by a city's or region's entrepreneurs. This operation proactively works to attract additional Community Audiences to join the branded Organic Environment.

Community Development Team – Recruits people from Community Audiences to become volunteers to support specific needs in the city or region, as well as to encourage other support programs and entrepreneur organizations to join the branded Organic Environment. Volunteer roles and entrepreneurial needs are communicated, in person, to people in the community as well as through the Media & Promotion Team.

10. Metrics Operation - Tracks the metrics for the nine other operations and entrepreneurial businesses working within each. From these metrics come insights for how to better help entrepreneurs and gain increased support from the community.

Metrics Team – Evaluates results from the nine other operations, the adoption of support programs, the progress of entrepreneurial businesses, and the support of the Community Audiences in terms of culture. High-level metrics are communicated to the community and Media and Promotion Team.

"The Metrics act as the compass to the Organic Environment's "GPS," providing the insights to understand how effectively entrepreneurs are being guided and how the community's culture is developing. The community coordinators leading the Metrics operation enables cities, like Kansas City, to better understand the entrepreneur community and how to increase their successes to grow the overall economy."

~ Jeff Kaczmarek

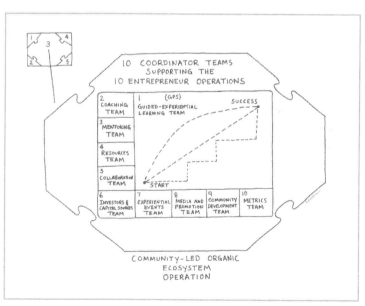

Community-Led Organic Environment:
10 Coordinating Teams support the 10 Entrepreneur Operations

A final team is the Administration Team made up exclusively of government and civic leaders who influence, support and offer perspectives to the coordinator teams. The Administrative Team does not have an operational function, but is instead positioned to help the coordinator teams gain the information they need to be as productive as possible.

Advisory Expert Matthew Hart is adamant that to achieve the desired entrepreneur, community and economic goals in 18 – 24 months requires an attentive Administrative Team. The Administrators' main roles are to support coordinators as they build the Organic Environment, ensure all teams are aware of their objectives, and help struggling teams push past obstacles. This sounds straightforward, but given the Entrepreneur and Community Social Infrastructures we discussed in previous chapters, Administrators have a tough balancing act to maintain. They have to own the outcome and be a fully engaged participant in the process, but can't steal free will or impinge on the community's or entrepreneurs' perception of ownership. Moreover, with 10 coordinator teams all having different action plans, there is a level of sophistication that requires remaining ardently team-focused. The **Servant Leader** model is critical here.

Coordinators will all make a significant time commitment, often volunteering as much as 20 hours a month. So it is crucial to remember the community mindsets when influencing or

> *"If the Organic Environment is to be the community's, then it must be theirs! The community and the coordinators can be influenced, but the control must be left in their hands! The community and the coordinators must "own" the success for it to be realized."*
>
> ~ *Michie P. Slaughter*

offering perspectives, to assure their continued involvement. An additional mindset is in play that only applies to coordinators: offering personal and community benefits simultaneously. Coordinators are business professionals, owners, or corporate employees who set aside hours for volunteering. Providing personal benefits may help coordinators visualize their volunteerism as complimenting their business or career interests. A coordinator may have an overarching business motivation in addition to a philanthropic reason for being involved.

> *"Keeping track of 10 programs simultaneously requires the right kind of organizer. Make sure you have the right combination of courage, diplomacy, flexibility, and decisiveness because coordination and calibration take energy and passion."*
>
> *~ Matthew Hart*

The coordinator for the Investor & Capital Sources Operation in the Grow Blue Springs Organic Environment (in Blue Springs, MO) is Kim Deveney. Kim owns American Funding Solutions, a factoring company that buys receivables of businesses that need cash in the short-term. Her business grows by providing factoring services to additional businesses. A benefit of Kim's coordinator role is that she is a resource to small businesses who are in need of capital, which in turn, results in Kim remaining engaged in the community. So it is critical for government and civic leaders to understand these dual motives for each coordinator. By keeping these two motivations in sync, even when the coordinator's business life experiences turbulence, he/she will stay engaged because their post may be the vehicle to a smoother business environment.

To review, the community-led organic environment is

designed to recruit Community Audiences to become coordinators and support the specific tasks required for success. As coordinators support each operation, it is important they are informed about and understand the entrepreneurial mindsets so they can effectively engage. This operation will provide the groundwork for the community to embrace entrepreneurship through volunteerism, and thereby shape the culture and accelerate economic growth!

"Its good for Communities to showcase entrepreneurial success. Entrepreneurs desire to start and grow businesses where they know they will be supported. So promote success and educate the community frequently and consistently!"

~Jo Anne Gabbert

Operation 4: Community-Focused Results

"Big results require big ambitions!" ~ Heraclitus

Community-focused results are a critical operation that reports on the progress of the community and Coordinator teams. Each coordinator team should report metrics, as defined by government and civic leaders. These metrics should measure the effectiveness of their communications, the gain in awareness and involvement from the community, and progress made within each team's entrepreneur operation focus. Reports can be either written or electronic, though information and insights can be accessed real-time via technology. (*Real-time information likely seems unnecessary, but when a community embraces the Organic Environment the pace of activity in the city or region will dramatically accelerate...equaling accelerated economic outcomes.*) Entrepreneurs and their support businesses, programs, and vendors will be evaluated and reported on through entrepreneur operations described in the next chapter: the Entrepreneur Operation Infrastructure.

Reporting on the community-focused results is as much a responsibility for the coordinator teams as it is for government and civic leaders. The information and insights gained from the reports are useful for distinct reasons to specific audiences:

For Government and Civic Leaders

- Identifies whether community communications, experiential events, and the coordinators and Community Audiences are creating positive change, which results in more support for entrepreneurship.

- Pinpoints what additional changes need to be made.
- Using the community mindsets, helps them know how to encourage these changes. *(The community reports will become very important as they are compared against the entrepreneur evaluations discussed in the next chapter.)*

For Coordinator Teams

- Tracks the outcomes their efforts are delivering in the community and for entrepreneurs.
- Helps identify what is working and how best to achieve greater outcomes.
- Offers continued motivation and inspiration for the value of volunteering.

For Community Audiences

- Reinforces that progress is being made to the economy from the changes people in the community are making.
- Showcases the safety and benefits the Organic Environment provides for entrepreneurs and the local economy.

Tracking community progress is another key difference between *The Organic Entrepreneur Economy*'s methodology and naturally-forming entrepreneur ecosystems. The Organic Environment methodology provides a systematic way to track the support structures available for entrepreneurs, not to mention how the entrepreneur ecosystem is being built and sustained. This key difference also recognizes the community as an active driver and participant in establishing entrepreneurship in a city or region, and not just part of the landscape. Therefore, being able to track and support the community, in addition to the entrepreneurs, is essential for any entrepreneur ecosystem. Without an Community Operational Infrastructure, it is very difficult to track community support or entrepreneurs at any level. Using the Community Operational Infrastructure as a framework for the Community Audiences, coordinator teams, and the corresponding Organic Environment makes tracking effortless.

"The benefits of reporting on the community's progress, its culture, and in fostering entrepreneurship is incredibly valuable. This opens up a whole new range of opportunities for leaders in evaluating their economic and community efforts."

~ Lisa Franklin

Clark Smith, a Principal at Smart Solutions Group, is an expert in consulting with government, civic and economic development organizations. He acknowledges that entrepreneurship is a massive opportunity that requires a widespread solution. Clark believes that the community is critical to the success of any initiative, especially an entrepreneurial one. Thus Clark has partnered with Evis Consulting and its Advisory Experts to help cities and regions realize the entrepreneurial and economic potential within their community. Clark admits that government and civic leaders reviewing the Organic Environment for the first time are often uncomfortable with the process, but he has found those same communities to be very supportive and quick to embrace the process once they get started. Since this system is grassroots and empowers the community to build their own future, the once-nervous leaders are reassured by the strengthening that occurs in their city or region. Clark and the other leaders utilizing the methodology are also in agreement that the operational integrity of supporting the community and entrepreneurs relies on a firm understanding of the mindsets.

Mindsets are incredibly valuable for understanding how the community will react and perceive requests to become involved. The entrepreneurial mindsets are also invaluable to coordinators in their work with business, support programs and vendors. So it is evident that understanding the psychology of the community and entrepreneurs is important. Without this knowledge, economic growth in a city or region would understandably seem unpredictable and uncontrollable, something most readers perceive when first reading this book.

"These results help leaders learn how the community's and entrepreneurs' mindsets are changing. This allows the community's Organic Environment to be regularly updated to meet the city or region's changing needs."

~ Lisa Franklin

So the community-focused results operation guides the reporting of progress in a community as more people become involved with the Organic Environment to support entrepreneurs and grow the local economy.

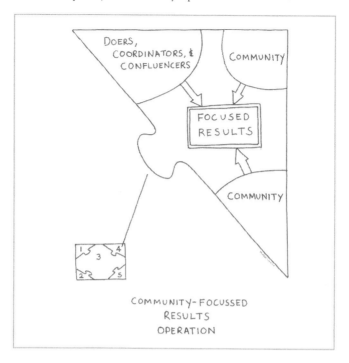

Community-Focused Results Operaiion

Operation 5: Community-Shared Empowerment

"If your actions inspire others to dream more, learn more, do more and become more, you are a leader."
~ *John Quincy Adams*

"Giving entrepreneurs a seat at the table is crucial to providing inside perspectives on what entrepreneurs need from their community leaders. Entrepreneurs can tell how the delivering mechanism for the support would best suit them. Communities that don't actively engage with their entrepreneurs spend much time and money trying to figure out what entrepreneurs want. You must communicate, activate and engage the entrepreneurs that are seen as leaders in your entrepreneurial community."

~Jo Anne Gabbert

Community-shared empowerment is a powerful operation that encourages people to support entrepreneurship and grow the economy in their own creative ways. This happens all the time in places like Silicon Valley and Boston, which have thriving entrepreneur ecosystems, but in cities and regions that don't yet have this established, it is not the case. However, as more communication reaches the community about its entrepreneurial successes and supportive culture and as more people meet their home-grown business owners...the creative energy will begin to flow. Early on this energy will be funneled into the community-branded Organic Environment. But as the proliferation and excitement of entrepreneurship spreads, the creativity begins to manifest in individual or group expressions of support. The occurrence of these expressions, referred to as social ventures, can take the form of collaborative groups, events, investor networks, incubators, co-working spaces, or any number of new support mechanisms.

The community-shared empowerment operation is an early indicator of organic acceleration, as the more people that decide to support entrepreneurship by launching a social venture the greater the capacity and draw there will be for these support mechanisms in the community. It is the start of a chain reaction of people being drawn in to help and start social ventures, fueled by communications to the community concerning entrepreneur success and support. People become excited by what is being accomplished for entrepreneurs and desire to become involved to further increase those accomplishments.

This started to occur in Kansas City about three years ago, from the writing of this book. People began to step forward to create social ventures, like the incubators: Innovation Cafe, BetaBlox, and LaunchKC

"Empowering additional programs and initiatives in the city or region is the most efficient method to achieve critical mass for entrepreneur and economic growth. The momentum for the Organic Environment's "engine" will create excitement and the perception of opportunity that will draw other social entrepreneurs in to offer mechanisms of support. Embracing these new mechanisms along with the Organic Environment will strengthen and grow the entrepreneurial community."

~ Jeff Kaczmarek

to name a few. For example, one of BetaBlox co-founder's Weston Bergmann, was inspired and confident that he could help fellow entrepreneurs start and grow their businesses by providing pods of about 10, increased access to training, mentors, and even investors. Think about that...Weston created an incubator in the Kansas City community which closely resembled a business startup as a mechanism to support entrepreneurs. He perceived this entrepreneurial need from what was communicated and through his interactions with the community. For government and city leaders, this translates into large numbers of people waiting to invest their money and time to create support mechanisms for their community.

"Entrepreneurs desire a sense of belonging. When venues and environments are created that foster this sense of belonging, relationships are built. These relationships generate entrepreneurial growth and development within communities."

~Jo Anne Gabbert

Brien Starner, President of the Blue Springs Economic Development Corporation and facilitator of GrowBlueSprings' Organic Environment, believes whole heartedly in empowering his community and coordinator teams to empower the community. At the time of writing this book, GrowBlueSprings has already embraced three events that have been created by people who see them as social ventures of sorts. Brien acknowledges that these events create a stronger and greater sense of community support for entrepreneurs, which can only help support the City of Blue Springs and the surrounding Jackson County region. Brien notes that while there are incubators in the city that at times overlap GrowBlueSprings' offerings, he views it as a positive way to increase the message that Blue Springs, Missouri is a supportive environment for entrepreneurs.

As new social ventures are launched, some may duplicate or overlap existing community operations in the Entrepreneur or Community Infrastructures. When this happens, and it will, the response should be to collaborate with the social venture to identify how to partner to enhance the community's Organic Environment. This may seem difficult, but coordinators are likely to spot these overlaps early and use their influence to find a collaborative route to move forward. It is crucial to understand that social ventures are essential for organic acceleration to occur and that the community's Organic Environment is the framework that allows for continued growth of the community, entrepreneurs, and economy. Unfortunately, without an Organic Environment or a community-wide framework, the entrepreneur ecosystem and economy is subject to constant cycles of speeding up and slowing down, due to periods of support and competition among social ventures. This is the reason why natural-forming economies and entrepreneur ecosystems are rarely able to reach the iconic levels of productivity of Silicon Valley or Boston.

"The Organic Environment and Infrastructures offer a comprehensive strategy for fostering entrepreneurship through the community. Without an integrated strategy, it can be difficult to extrapolate how the success of community or entrepreneur programs affect an entire city or region's economy. The Organic Environment really does provide an insider's perspective into fostering an entrepreneur community in a city or region!"

~ Lisa Franklin

To ensure that the community-shared empowerment operation is effective in generating a sustainable Organic Environment for the community, the following tasks must be achieved:

- Coordinator teams engage with social ventures and regularly communicate progress within the community.

- Regular interaction with people throughout the community occurs to encourage involvement, entrepreneurship and social ventures.

- Support is shown for entrepreneurs and social ventures who fail, and others in the community are encouraged to show the same support. *(Remember the Overcoming Failures community mindset applies to social ventures as well.)*

Achieving the three tasks of the community-shared empowerment generates activity within the community and greatly increases its chances for organic acceleration. So essentially community-shared empowerment is the effect of the excitement building in the community from the perception of entrepreneurial growth in the city or region. This powerful operation occurs as people in the community perceive progress in their branded Organic Environment. The occurrence of this operation indicates that achieving organic acceleration for the community and of the entrepreneur ecosystem is close at hand.

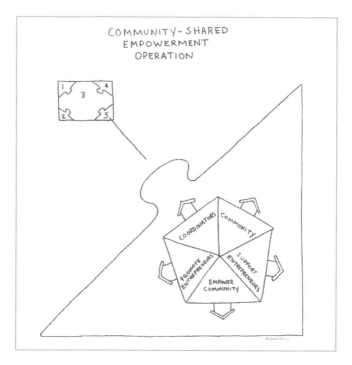

Community-Shared Empowerment Operation

Community Operational Infrastructure Review

The Community Operational Infrastructure details the five operations that must be accomplished by government and civic leaders, Community Audiences, and coordinator teams to organically foster a supportive culture, increase entrepreneurial activity and grow the economy. This infrastructure depicts how community perceptions, involvement and empowerment are essential to achieving organic acceleration. Thus before government and civic leaders can influence their community to opera-

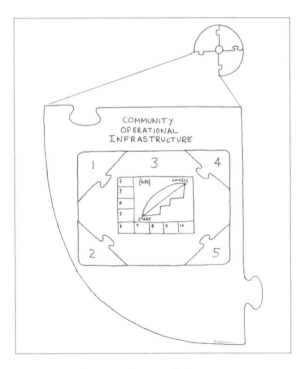

Community Operational Infrastructure

tionally engage, they must first understand the community and entrepreneurial mindsets. Only when a community-wide framework is in place can a city or regional economy be stabilized and grown. Hence the community truly is the key and point of engagement required for the stabilization and growth of any economy!

"This operation has no doubt demonstrated the immense, and often untapped, economic energy that is available through engaging the community. Utilizing the community significantly accelerates the potential and speed for growing the economy and fostering widespread entrepreneurship."

~ Dr. Bernard Franklin

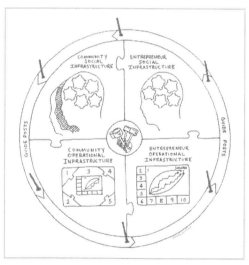

The complete *Organic Entrepreneur Economy*:
Organic Environment, four Infrastructures and 6 Guideposts

Chapter 8:

The Entrepreneur Operational Infrastructure

Early on, Larry Lee pointed out the struggle in Kansas City of how to support entrepreneurial masses while still focusing on the most promising businesses. Based on the Kauffman Foundation's Index for Entrepreneurial Activity, statistically 2,500 new entrepreneurial ventures should be created each month in the Kansas City region based upon its population. Against that metric, government and civic leaders only knew of about 100 to 200 business creations each year, mostly from university programs or incubators. Supporting those few hundred businesses was consuming most of the budgeted resources allotted for entrepreneurship. The most obvious solution, though seemingly impossible, was to build a personalized incubation assembly line of sorts that could support the 2,500+ new entrepreneurs that should be starting up each month in Kansas City, not to mention helping the larger number of growing businesses!

Jeff Kaczmarek, then President and CEO of Kansas City's Economic Development Corporation, knew these facts and desired a better way to support all entrepreneurial potential. We realized that if support programs were linked together based on an entrepreneur's stage of growth, then the pre-existing programs in Kansas City would become an assembly line, preparing and screening the entrepreneur for the next needed program. This would allow the entrepreneurial masses to join any program in the "network" to become connected to a city-wide "pod". Their commitment and progress would become the mechanism for admittance to the other programs.

Jeff pointed out that while it should work in theory, most programs were not designed to handle constant demand from hundreds or thousands of entrepreneurs at one time. He was also concerned about what would drive entrepreneurs forward through the programs. That is when we agreed to overlay an experiential learning curriculum similar to a road map to guide entrepreneurs through the stages of starting or growing their businesses. Additionally events and investor connections were proposed as incentives for entrepreneurs to stay engaged.

"It is paramount that the community perceives that they are engaged and have some control of and influence on their entrepreneur operation. Even though this is atypical, it will instill a level of confidence that propels the community to become more confident of their businesses and purposeful in growing their economy. This approach instills a sense of community: collaboration instead of competition!"

~ Brien M. Starner

This was the moment Jeff realized that Kansas City had a strategy to support its entrepreneurs. The stages of Guided, Experiential Learning addressed the most significant steps that entrepreneurs needed to take, and then connected them to the network of support programs, vendors, and other services for further development. Thus we could avoid building a system to replace existing support program providers and instead unify existing programs into a collective network. Jeff agreed with the direction, but insisted that this operation needed to be clearly defined to be successful, and needed to support and connect existing providers without hindering them. It needed to be tracked, and if possible, the entire operation run by the community...as he perceived there was not available staff to support it at the governmental level.

So this is where the 10 operations of the Entrepreneur Operations Infrastructure come into play:

1. Guided, Experiential Learning

2. Coaching

3. Mentoring

4. Resources

5. Collaboration

6. Investors and Capital Sources

7. Experiential Events

8. Media and Promotion

9. Community Development

10. Metrics

The creation and implementation of the Entrepreneur Operational Infrastructure was validated quickly. In fact, entrepreneur Kerry Duffin had been a restaurateur and special events coordinator for years, but was looking to build a startup in the fashion industry, called lm brands. Interestingly Kerry knew lots of entrepreneurs that could mentor him, but was missing the "GPS" that aggregated the necessary startup information in

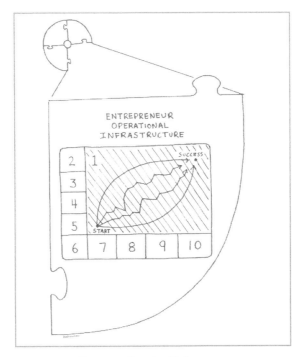

Entreprenur Operational Infrastructure

an organized format for his new venture. Kerry asked us to help him with this, but insisted that he wanted to make all of decisions. We warned him that if we did, his actions and successes would dictate the amount of support he received. Kerry looked at us perplexed and said, "Isn't that the way it's supposed to be?"

The value of the Entrepreneur Operational Infrastructure in providing a path, or "GPS," for entrepreneurs to navigate starting up or growing a business is just the beginning. For government and city leaders, it is the ability to track the progress of hundreds, if not thousands, of businesses while effortlessly directing entrepreneurs to support programs, vendors and community members.

As you explore each of the ten operations, it is important to remember how the entrepreneurial mindsets are at play to create engagement. Think about the support programs in your city or region that could easily fit into each operation.

"Entrepreneurs need guidance and resources that fit their needs...not just those offering to help. This great conundrum can be overcome through experientially guiding entrepreneurs to identify what is needed on their own...and having solutions available when they do!"

~ Corey J. Mehaffy

Operation 1: Guided, Experiential Learning

"I hear and I forget. I see and I remember. I do and I understand." ~ *Confucius*

Guided, Experiential Learning is an entrepreneurial learning style where skills and insights are taught through situational experiences. The **guided** style provides entrepreneurs with insights and skills they need WHILE growing their business. Training follows the business cycle, instead of being completed prior to business start-up. In this way, the sequential format helps entrepreneurs self-realize the training, resources, and support needs they have at each stage of their business development. It is important to remember the five entrepreneurial mindsets, as these must be adhered to for the Guided, Experiential Learning to be effective and utilized.

It is important to note that while experiential learning is becoming a popular technique for skills training or to provide a perspective, it is rarely used as an active guide for starting or growing a business. Experiential learning works by replicating a scenario, usually in a controlled environment, that teaches the trainee through experience. This technique allows entrepreneurs to learn multiple skills and insights at pre-defined stages of the business development cycle.

This is incredibly difficult, costly to set up and implement, and requires a significant investment of time. There are a few incubators across the country which are able to achieve this technique in small entrepreneur class sizes of 10-20 at a time. To help cities and regions, the Organic Environment needed the potential to do this in much larger class sizes and with a fraction of the time and financial costs. This was nearly the end of the Organic Environment, until the Advisory Experts realized that the 50 or so entrepreneurs they interviewed in the beginning had a common process for starting and growing a business that could be used as a template, or path, for guiding the experiential learning. With that knowledge, two pre-defined paths were constructed to guide the sequential experiential learning needed to startup or grow a business.

"It truly was a feat to understand entrepreneurs and build a guide to proactively lead them through the challenges that they would face. By utilizing Experiential learning, entrepreneurs were able to understand what and how business worked by experiencing the actions on their business. This really is the only approach for providing intimate and viable training to a community's entrepreneurial masses!"

~ Danny Lobina

This approach gained credibility in Kansas City by one of the earliest contributors to *The Organic Entrepreneur Economy*, Joe Mullins. Joe, a serial entrepreneur and consultant with the University of Central Missouri, regularly led training sessions on how to start a business. The training guided entrepreneurs through the process of idea generation, prototyping, gaining sales, reading financials, and undertaking other business start-up components in a quick 6-10 week course. Joe observed that entrepreneurs understand the concepts in the classroom, but would quickly become bogged down when putting knowledge into action. *(For example, as the entrepreneur attempted to solve existing challenges and further developed the business, he or she altered the business model and strategy. This in turn evolved the business, but created new opportunities and challenges that required more training. While this may seem like a healthy and natural process, it required significant amounts of the entrepreneur's time to enroll and take classes to learn what to do next.)* He found that entrepreneurs were constantly in need of additional skills and knowledge, but rarely knew it.

Joe asserted early on in the creation of Kansas City's Organic Environment that there needed to be "navigational" training available to directionally guide entrepreneurs to self-realize what to do when starting or growing a business. Joe surmised that this could then lead to providing entrepreneurs access to skills training, resources, investors, coaches, mentors, and other support programs needed at specific stages in their business creation or growth.

Joe realized that when entrepreneurs engaged in Guided, Experiential Learning through the startup or growth paths, they consistently came to the specific realizations - on their own - based on the stage of their business. For instance:

1. What step to do next

2. Which tasks are required to complete each step

3. What insights or skills do they lack to achieve the next step

4. What training, resources and capital do they need to achieve the step

5. How this step fits into the path that leads to business success

Think about that for a moment... these self-realizations put the entrepreneurs in charge of the 5 mindsets and ensures the entrepreneurs perceive control *(in picking of vendors and choosing which business steps to take)* and allows them to take charge of simultaneously learning, developing and growing their business. *(Additionally*

"Most of the time, entrepreneurs don't know what they don't know. And it takes a "learning experience" for the entrepreneur to realize what they don't know. Thus having a guide to rapidly help entrepreneur overcome this block in knowledge is invaluable!"

~ Michie P. Slaughter

"Entrepreneurs long for a roadmap to success. They tend to seek others who have "been there, done that" as a means to learn about the road others have traveled. Every community needs successful entrepreneurs to be mentors that are willing to share their road to success."

~ Jo Anne Gabbert

this approach provides vendors of training and support programs a pipeline of entrepreneurial customers.) Thus Guided, Experiential Learning becomes the cornerstone of the Organic Environment.

The Guided, Experiential Learning operation utilizes two forms of entrepreneurial learning: 1) Paths and 2) Business Training. Paths provide the entrepreneur "navigational" directions for how to startup or grow a business. Business training provides specific industry training (i.e. lean manufacturing or biotech compliance) and skill-specific training (i.e. sales, marketing, or accounting training) to entrepreneurs as they traverse the paths. Further the two forms of training work hand-in-hand and are complementary to each other in the Organic Environment. Paths are maintained by the Guided, Experiential Coordinator Team from within the Community Operational Infrastructure. Business training vendors are maintained by the businesses that offer them in the city or region. This keeps the two trainings from overlapping and vendors from vying for power.

Paths

The Guided, Experiential Learning paths were again built from the experiences of roughly 50 serially successful entrepreneurs in Kansas City and around the country who described strikingly similar business startup and growth processes. Based on these detailed descriptions, we compiled a list of sequential stages and steps needed to start or grow a business. This resulted in two paths: StartPath and GrowPath. The difficult part of designing the paths was translating the skills and insights needed at each business development stage into an activity that produces the intended experience and learning for entrepreneurs.

Moreover, the StartPath and GrowPath were each built based on the feedback from 50 entrepreneurs from multiple industries, having unique market focuses, representing different businesses types and demonstrating varying degrees of experience and skills. So the paths needed to mirror this broad spectrum in order to serve a city's or region's diverse entrepreneurial masses. Correctly building the startup and growth paths to ensure that a broad range of entrepreneurs could successfully utilize the Guided, Experiential Learning took substantial attention to the five entrepreneurial mindsets and years of refinement.

"The Organic Environment's approach for guiding entrepreneurs through startup and growth using the experiences of successful entrepreneurs is an incredibly valuable tool. This tool will undoubtedly accelerate startup and growth for businesses as it directs them to the activities that are most valuable for them and helps them to avoid many mistakes that are naturally made."

~ Christopher Doroh

The format for the two paths - StartPath and GrowPath - focused on unique types of entrepreneurial activities and experiences. Since entrepreneurs work at all times of day and night, it was critical these paths are available 24/7/365. In Kansas City, this required building a web portal that was "always on" and ready to support the activity of any entrepreneur...much like a virtual incubator.

StartPath guides aspiring entrepreneurs from idea to a revenue-generating business, connecting them just-in-time to support programs, services, vendors, coaches, mentors, and investors when the entrepreneur recognizes a need. The StartPath focus for entrepreneurs must be on 1) achieving revenues as fast as possible, and 2) screening aspiring entrepreneurs based on their ability to commit to the work needed to reach viability. These two focuses are the critical outcomes required for a business to achieve viability. A positive side-effect is that it guides aspiring entrepreneurs to self-realize early if their idea is not viable or they are unwilling to make the intense work hours commitment. This is valuable as it results in the entrepreneur self-realizing the need for strategic shifts in their idea or business plan, or for those unwilling to make the time commitment, recognize the need to quit early before making substantial investments. Both these possible outcomes can be construed as being forms of success.

The GrowPath guides a business with early revenues to employ systems and processes to create a more scalable and sustainable business. It also connects just-in-time to the support programs, services, vendors, coaches, mentors, investors, and everything else required when the entrepreneur recognizes a need. The GrowPath focus needs to be on the systems and processes necessary to increase business profits and ability to achieve further success as defined by the entrepreneur. *(It is important to remember that every entrepreneur will define success differently and not all success results*

> *"The fact that entrepreneurial startups are so lucrative to an economy is one that all economic development and governmental leaders should be excited about. It is disconcerting that much of this business is leaving through the web. This should entice all leaders to evaluate how to keep those millions in "entrepreneur stimulus" within the community and should be a wake up call for those who are not directing significant resources into fostering local entrepreneurship!"*
>
> *~ Dr. Bernard Franklin*

in greater revenues or employee counts. Sometimes it is more about time availability or fulfilling a passion. The focus must be solely on the entrepreneur's definition of success!)

The strength of both paths is the ability to gain training, skills, and support in a "just-in-time" format when a need is self-realized...not when the entrepreneur is told there is a need. Resources, collaboration, events, investors, mentors, coaches, and other support programs are spread throughout the paths to provide entrepreneurs access when needed. These strengths reduce the time required to startup and grow businesses, as entrepreneurs now have the mechanisms to self-realize needs and bring the qualified connections to them. This is especially useful, as roughly 70% of small business owners have day jobs, so their needs are often faced and addressed on weekends and in the evenings. The paths are especially significant in this instance, as these entrepreneurs are likely to search online, which in turn will deprive city and regional resource, support programs, and vendors of revenue. These revenues will add up to losses in the millions of dollars for cities and regions...even in populations as small as 15,000 people.

For government and civic leaders, the paths provide a funnel for supporting, tracking and measuring startups and growing businesses. The paths should be built in an online format along with the other nine program operations, allowing constant access for entrepreneurs and creating the potential for real-time reporting. In Kansas City, this tracking provided significant understandings for what entrepreneurs were lacking and how they were struggling. The paths made it possible to simultaneously support large numbers of entrepreneurs at any given time and still intimately promote their activities through the support of the coordinator teams.

Business Training

For both StartPath and GrowPath, it is incredibly valuable inserting traditional business training, or seminars, that teach industry knowledge or skills. The paths guide entrepreneurs to self-realize or become aware of the needs and additional knowledge required at each stage of their developing business. The business training programs and vendors that already exist in a city or region can be experientially placed within each path. Each placement should 1) describe what the training solves, so the entrepreneur can connect the training solution with a realized need, and 2) a registration link to signup for the program or seminar.

> *"It is critical to have businesses and community leaders connected to a city or region's education leaders to influence collaboration and support for entrepreneurial learning in K-12 schools, colleges and universities, as well as adult education. Then the community can be trained to see the value and outcomes from experiential learning!"*
>
> *~Michie P. Slaughter*

With business start-up and growth, it is always important to know your target market and customers. To most entrepreneurs this means going online and learning as much as possible about the market, what customers are buying, and how potential competitors successfully engage those customers. In the United States, this is the approach we were taught in school. These paths and training programs logically begin to assist entrepreneurs identifying their markets in a way that can actually help them sell to customers at the same time. For instance, in an early stage of StartPath, an entrepreneur experientially self-realizes who the customer base is by reaching out to 30 people perceived to be in the target market and who they don't know. The entrepreneurs then describe their product/service and ask these three simple questions:

1. Would you buy the product/service?

2. How much would you pay?

3. Can I have the money now as a down-payment?

I bet you can imagine the responses that come from this activity, the realizations that entrepreneurs gain, and how this may actually generate a customer! This often helps entrepreneurs realize that they need training on how to better market or sell their product/service, which is a realization that entrepreneurs rarely come to early on. So the paths create the *"Oh Crap!"* moment that help entrepreneurs come to self-realizations. At this point, they often realize they need assistance and reach out for further training and support program vendor help.

> *"Oh Crap realizations are personal moments of clarity for entrepreneurs. Ironically, just because an entrepreneur gains clarity for what needs to be done, doesn't mean they will have the tools or resources to achieve it. So having the paths connect entrepreneurs to these tools and resources is very valuable."*
>
> ~ *Steve Meinzen*

In this way, the paths become pipelines, guiding entrepreneurs to realize their need for industry or skill-specific training and then connecting them directly to the city's or region's vendors. Additionally this approach allows the entrepreneur to reach out to the training vendor as a partner in overcoming obstacles while perceiving complete control over the five mindsets. This is in opposition to entrepreneurs who pushback when training vendors point out seemingly, obvious weaknesses in their business. Moreover, this approach ensures the paths are not in competition with the city's or region's training vendors, but rather become an opportunity for the community's vendors.

The result of utilizing both paths and business training within the Guided, Experiential Learning is that the operation becomes the conduit for:

"Business training is a huge benefit for any business seeking new skills or knowledge. Paths provide entrepreneurs a "GPS" guide of step-by-step instructions on how to start and grow businesses. Essentially, paths fill in the blanks or gaps for entrepreneurs and help them to understand the skills and knowledge they need to be trained on. Paths don't compete with training, but instead increase connectivity and the demand for business training. This is an important pairing for entrepreneurs and their community."

~ Barry J Crocker

1. Entrepreneurs to have a one-stop guide for starting and growing their businesses.

2. Support program vendors which gain a pipeline that connects them with entrepreneurs who recognize their value and are ready to purchase from them.

3. Government and civic leaders who gain tracking and metrics throughout the startup or growth business lifecycles, as well as clarity for how entrepreneurs are engaging and benefiting from the training programs.

The Guided, Experiential Learning operation guides entrepreneurs through business startup or growth and channels them to the business training vendors needed along the way. This conduit is the gateway that screens and connects entrepreneurs to the nine additional operations. The Guided, Experiential Learning operation fits within the Entrepreneur Operational Infrastructure as depicted in the diagram.

"Entrepreneurs do not have much respect for institutions, educators, or corporate executives who offer training, until they realize a need. Thus it is critical to provide training at the precise time an entrepreneur has a need, called "Just-in-Time" learning."

~ Michie P. Slaughter

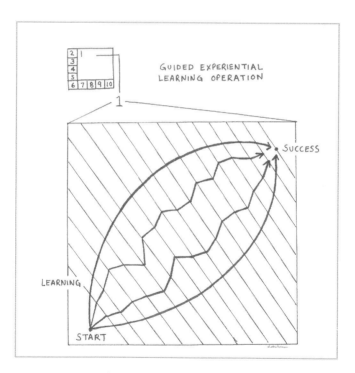

Guided Experiential Learning Operation

Operation 2: Coaching

"Catch a man a fish, Feed him for a day. Teach him how to fish, And feed him for life." ~ Unknown

Coaches are typically sounding boards for entrepreneurs, as well as providers of insights and advice. Coaches can be business consultants, certified business or life coaches, coaches from existing programs, or even coaches from government's Small Business Development Centers or similar federally-backed programs in the city or region.

"Coaches are screened by coordinators within the Organic Environment, but there should also be additional screening for networks and track records. These coaches will be critical guides in giving insights and connections to the city or region's entrepreneurs when they need it most."

~ Jo Anne Gabbert

Within the Entrepreneur Operational Infrastructure and Guided, Experiential Learning paths, the coaches' operational importance is much greater as they guide entrepreneurs through the stages of startup and growth. Coaches are chosen at the beginning of each path by the entrepreneur to personalize the experiential learning and guidance and to allow for perspectives to be industry-specific. The coach also acts as a secondary screening mechanism when entrepreneurs request connections to mentors, investors and events. These three operations (Mentors, Investors and Capital Sources, and Experiential Events) need qualified entrepreneurs, and the coach is the mechanism to both screen and connect entrepreneurs to them...reducing the traditional time and financial costs accrued by a business owner. This works because the coach's reputation benefits from being the entrepreneur's "agent" and by granting them access to their perceived needs.

A coach also ensures that the entrepreneur completes the necessary stages in the respective path, meets a prescribed set of requirements, is prepared to effectively interact with desired mentors, investors and capital sources, and be able to present at events. The coach's reputation and his/her ability to help entrepreneurs *(in the instance where a connected entrepreneur is not prepared)* is affected when coordinators or the mentors, investors, and event hosts deny or block future connections. This creates a set of checks and balances for coaches, and ensures that only screened entrepreneurs are passed along to the desired contacts.

The operational beauty of using coaches is that it drastically reduces the amount of time and busy work for coaching coordinators and government and civic administrators. It also provides a secondary screening mechanism, behind the Guided, Experiential Learning paths, to ensure entrepreneurs are motivated to progress through the stages of development towards their defined success. This allows entrepreneurs to stay focused on starting or growing their business, instead of focusing on time-intensive tasks of finding resources and service vendors, mentors, guidance, additional capital sources, or simply how to solve the next

> *"Integrating coaches as connectors for entrepreneurs streamlines the process of ensuring that new and growing businesses are validated and screened. This operation will increase the overall attractiveness of the city or region's entrepreneurial businesses from an investor's or other strategic partner's perspective."*
>
> ~ Danny Lobina

unknown problem.

Coaches are needed to guide the entrepreneur and provide context within the paths. The coach can become a trusted advisor for the entrepreneur, helping him/her work through getting stuck or perceiving a lack of control. Coaches can also act as customer service representatives when there are problems, as they are trusted by the entrepreneur, community, and vendors.

> "Great coaches and mentors are experts in directing entrepreneurs to the resources and training they need before they realize it. Coaches and mentors must have a network of resources to offer entrepreneurs if they are to become an asset and trusted advisor to them."
>
> ~ Jo Anne Gabbert

Shawn Kinkade is President of Aspire Business Development and a certified business coach. Shawn is one of the best coaches in Kansas City and has guided many emerging entrepreneurs through the business development process. Shawn believes the best way to work with entrepreneurs is by guiding them to the answer rather than simply telling it to them. This is an aspect of entrepreneurship that business owners will only value once they have experienced it. Shawn hosts mastermind groups and events to let entrepreneurs experience coaching and gain appreciation for it. Shawn's efforts are heroic and serve as the model for our coaching operation. Using that should allow another city or regional coach to achieve the same success.

Thus coaches moved from a "nice to have," to an essential connector between an entrepreneur and the community. In their new capacity, coaches help government and civic leaders better connect and direct their entrepreneurs to the many resources in the city or region, while ensuring their clients' businesses are appropriately prepared and positioned for development or growth. The coaching operation fits within the Entrepreneur Operational Infrastructure as described in the diagram.

"The Organic Environment increases the value coaches have with and for entrepreneurs, without hindering their ability to advise and counsel. Coaches instinctively screen entrepreneurs so they are ready for business opportunities, making the process within the Organic Environment completely natural!"

~ Danny Lobina

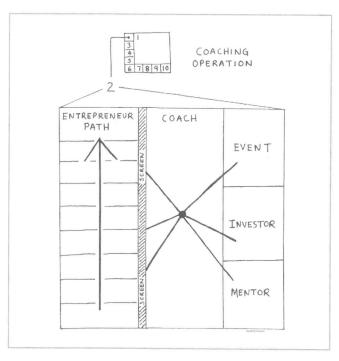

Coaching Operation

Operation 3: Mentoring

"Mentoring is a brain to pick, an ear to listen, and a push in the right direction." ~ John C. Crosby

The mentoring operation provides entrepreneurs opportunities to meet with experts in their market or industry that can provide insights, share experiences, and connections to help their business grow faster, more efficiently, and avoid common pitfalls. Mentors are often successful entrepreneurs, corporate executives, or industry experts. Mentoring also provides successful entrepreneurs with an opportunity to support the next generation of entrepreneurs and be recognized for it. This seemingly insignificant offer of recognition ensures that successful entrepreneurs help the next generation of business owners achieve success, as they perceive a gain in influence in the community by doing so. Thus by being recognized for the entrepreneurs they mentor, the community will view the mentee's business as a credit to the successful mentor's abilities. The communication and promotion of entrepreneurs and their mentors is done at events, in the media, and by the Mentor Coordinator Team.

"Entrepreneurs are inherently private, especially when failing. The key is helping them understand there are others that can help, even in the hard times. Mentors and coaches within the community provide the help and guidance needed to work through the difficulties each entrepreneur faces."

~ Danny Lobina

Jo Anne Gabbert, a serial entrepreneur and owner of JAG Portfolio Services, is constantly being tapped as a mentor for businesses and projects...including for *The Organic Entrepreneur Economy*. Jo Anne is a strong believer in the value mentors provide to entrepreneurs, but also believes there is an inherent need to screen mentors...as not all mentors are created equal! Ensuring entrepreneurs are getting accurate and usable advice is critical for the success of these businesses and the community. This screening process will identify what, if anything, the mentor hopes to garner from the relationship with an entrepreneur. Regardless of whether the mentor seeks public notoriety, to strengthen the economy, or something else, government, civic leaders and the coordinator team will know how to support the mentors...as much as the entrepreneurs!

In many cities, this is often a reality as the "Good 'Ole Boy Network" was always a little leery of helping younger entrepreneurs for fear that they might become or be perceived as more successful. Thus the Organic Environment provides a mechanism to celebrate and promote the mentors' support of entrepreneurs, empowering more successful business owners to become mentors. In turn, this empowerment offers the entrepreneurs a more involved and engaged mentor that is incentivized to help them succeed! Entrepreneurs gain an experienced, unpaid partner to provide critical insights as their Guided, Experiential Learning paths and coaches work them through the stages of developing their startup or growing business.

In the mentoring operation, mentors should be asked to outline their ideal mentee, which can be given to the coordinator team...to be matched against the mentee profiles submitted later by the coaches. When a coach

"Mentors are incredibly valuable to entrepreneurs, as they have many hard-fought successes under their belt that entrepreneurs can learn from. It is important to ensure that mentor involvement is recognized publicly as much as possible. This publicity will also strengthen the community's Organic Environment and increase the support of entrepreneurs."

~ Christopher Doroh

has an entrepreneur in need of mentoring, and has completed an outline of the corresponding business, it is sent to the Mentor coordinator team to assign a matching mentor. Upon identifying a match, the mentor is then given the option to meet the entrepreneur to discuss the desired topics. *(If the mentor denies the meeting, then another mentor is matched and offered the chance to meet.)*

Again, to entice strong participation among established and successful entrepreneurs, mentors should be recognized along with the entrepreneurs they advise at experiential events, in the media, and at every appropriate opportunity. Mentoring is value-added and critically utilized in StartPath and Grow-Path. The mentoring operation fits within the Entrepreneur Operational Infrastructure as can be seen in the diagram.

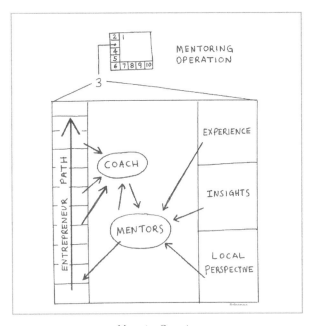

Mentoring Operation

Operation 4: Resources

"When every physical and mental resource is focused, one's power to solve a problem multiplies tremendously."

~ *Norman Vincent Peale*

Resources are the support programs, tools, and services *(such as lawyers, accounting programs, software development, etc.)* that entrepreneurs need when starting or growing their business. Entrepreneurs often perceive these resources to be *"nice-to-have"* wants, causing resource vendors to struggle with finding entrepreneurs who realize the need for the support programs, tools, or services. The result is a turbulent and confusing connection process between entrepreneurs and resource vendors. Moreover, many for-profit resource vendors are leery of startups that may not be able to pay their bills. However the validity of this stigma has been refuted by the statistics that the average startup spends $24,700 in their first year alone.

This $24,700 per startup is very important for government and civic leaders, as it can become a driver of economic growth. If entrepreneurs are connected to the city and regional resources, then this money will flow into support businesses in the community. Additionally the Kauffman

"The demand for resources by businesses is an early indicator of economic growth. Business creation and growth drives up the demand for local products and services, assuming the internet is not piping that demand outside of the city or region. Resource providers are likely many of the staple businesses in the community, and ensuring real-time connectivity and high demand increases the economic potential for the community."

~ *Dr. Bernard Franklin*

Foundation's Index of Entrepreneurial Activity shows that as of 2012 on average there are 300 new startups each month per population of 100,000 people. This alone can become an annual multi-million dollar stimulus package for a city or region! So this showcases the need for government and civic leaders to make sure their city's or region's resources are visible. The Organic Environment achieves this within the two paths and with the coaches, so entrepreneurs are able to seamlessly connect with these resources.

As roughly 75% of small business entrepreneurs have day jobs, the search for resources often occurs in the evening hours and on weekends. City and regional resource vendors must be more visible and more easily accessible to entrepreneurs during these hours, as they are competing with online search engines. It appears, however, that most cities and regions are not effectively connecting their entrepreneurs to their community's resources. Thus it is no surprise that nearly 70% of entrepreneurs rely on online search engines to find their resources. This also means that the money that could potentially stimulate businesses in a city or region is leaving to stimulate the businesses in other cities or regions; *and I bet those communities your city is stimulating won't even know it or say thank you!*

While entrepreneurs most often utilize online search engines when they have a problem, they will occasionally ask for suggestions or help from Small Business Technology Development Centers (SBTDC). Danny Lobina, the Director of the SBTDC in the Moberly-area Community College, has often seen how entrepreneurs value external providers over those in their city or region. This phenomenon reaches beyond just resources, but there is a perception that resource providers that are lesser known but have attractive materials are more credible and more effective. This guides many entrepreneurs away from the best resources that are available to help them, as those in their city or region likely provide a comparable product or service AND know how to deliver it to the advantage of local businesses. Danny regularly directs entrepreneurs to these "hometown" resources, and has seen significantly more progress in businesses that follow the advice. Hometown providers not only have the knowledge and solution, but also a desire to help entrepreneurs succeed in their city or region.

So it is critical to have a city's or region's resources organized in a way that allows the entrepreneurs to learn about each vendor when they have self-realized their need. Only having lists of resources, which we call "yellow pages roulette," is effectively useless, for entrepreneurs rarely understand what their problems are and so aren't seeking a vendor or the solution. If entrepreneurs could instantly recognize their problems, then a resource listing would make sense, and there wouldn't be any need for coaches or mentors to aid in starting or growing a business. We know this simply isn't the case.

"Using paths to guide entrepreneurs to resources is similar to how they are guided to business training. Entrepreneurs often have gaps in their knowledge or require additional insights to know what solution and service they require. So the paths help entrepreneurs self-realize their business needs, which provides an opportunity to connect them to resource providers in the city or region. This ensures that money spent on resources goes to local or regional providers."

~ Barry J Crocker

Thus entrepreneurs must be guided through experiences and self-realizations when resources are needed, directed towards city or regional vendors, and provided a portal for easy and constant access to learn about and connect with those resource vendors. *(The Organic Environment utilizes the Resource coordinator team to help attract and organize the resources and vendors.)* So the importance of the Resource operation, within the Entrepreneur Operational Infrastructure, is depicted in the diagram.

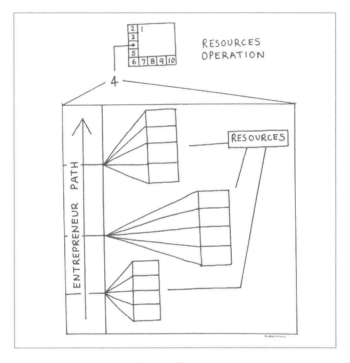

Resources Operation

Operation 5: Collaboration

"Alone we can do so little; together we can do so much"
~ Helen Keller

Collaboration is often considered to be a natural process when entrepreneurs interact naturally. Though in reality, collaboration is a powerful interaction that helps entrepreneurs learn through interactions with their peers. Originally in Kansas City, collaboration occurred as entrepreneurs formed their informal pods and gathered together to get their businesses unstuck or to discuss a critical business decision. Collaborating when the entrepreneur is stuck is good, but its better to collaborate constantly to gain insights that help a business from ever getting stuck.

"Entrepreneurs are often leery of collaboration because they fear someone might steal their idea. Coaches and mentors should stress that collaboration is the key to survival. Going it alone no longer works."

~Jo Anne Gabbert

So we began to collaborate with multiple groups to help set up venues in the form of groups, events, incubators, and co-working spaces. A more notable collaboration is the Entrepreneur Roundtable, co-founded by myself and other Kansas City entrepreneurs, and is a place for entrepreneurs to collaborate on their businesses and get insights from others in the group, as well as from expert speakers. The co-working space, Innovation Cafe, that was started as an extended office space for art dealer David Teeman, had a similar purpose. David bought a space as an office, and using his entrepreneurial spirit, sought to bring additional entrepreneurs in to sublease the space and to collaborate with. The Innovation Cafe is now the home to more than 100 entrepreneurs who work and collaborate on a daily basis! While the collaboration in both of these examples is very open-ended, visionaries like venture capitalist Herb Sih of Think Big Partners has an incubator and co-working space in which he uses collaboration to purposefully create business strategies, bring together investors and entrepreneurs, and help connect co-founders to entrepreneurs. Herb uses collaboration a bit more purposefully than most.

> "In-person interactions and collaborations are essential for entrepreneurs and the community. Face-to-face collaborations allow entrepreneurs the opportunity to gain more from feedback and camaraderie. I am a strong believer in having a virtual "always on" environment complimented by a physical space, offering entrepreneurs the most efficient and supportive environment possible."
>
> ~ Mark W. Dickey

In this same way, the Entrepreneur Operational Infrastructure utilizes collaboration to connect entrepreneurs in a community. The Guided, Experiential Learning paths add context to the topics and business stages that entrepreneurs may need to collaborate on. Ideally, with real-time metrics and reporting, the paths can pinpoint the businesses that are struggling and provide collaboration opportunities for overcoming their current challenges. Through the Organic Environment entrepreneurs can then be directed to engagement opportunities within an operation or within the city's or region's incubators, co-working spaces, or other collaboration venues. The collaboration coordinator team can organically aggregate the organizations and venues in a city or region to create a more connected environment for entrepreneurs.

Again, the purpose of the collaboration operation is to build a sense of camaraderie and confidence with entrepreneurs. Entrepreneurship is often a lonely profession, but the passion and energy that is generated when business owners interact motivates, encourages, and creates an informal mechanism of accountability for each business. Moreover, entrepreneurs are likely to identify their greatest challenges and gain context when collaborating with fellow entrepreneurs from their city or region. Thus the collaboration operation is a very important part of the Guided, Experiential Learning process and can support the entrepreneurs progression in StartPath or GrowPath when paired correctly with their business stage and experience.

The collaboration operation cultivates business owner and community interactions to reinvigorate the entrepreneur and support their progression in StartPath or GrowPath. The placement of the collaboration operation within the Entrepreneur Operational Infrastructure is described in the diagram.

"Entrepreneurs learn the most from successful entrepreneurs. Many people venture out from their corporate jobs into entrepreneurial endeavors only to find that their corporate experience isn't applicable to entrepreneurship. Seeking a community of like-minded entrepreneurs accelerates the new entrepreneur's learning curve"

~ Jo Anne Gabbert

"Collaborating with fellow entrepreneurs is the preferred method of learning for entrepreneurs, especially when the collaboration takes place in a safe and confidential group setting. This is a place where entrepreneurs can admit what they don't understand to receive unbiased support and insights!"

~ Michie P. Slaughter

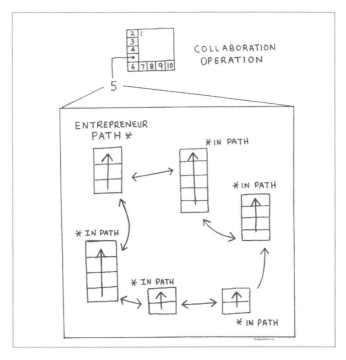

Collaboration Operation

Operation 6: Investors and Capital Sources

"Nothing turns off an investor more than when an entrepreneur comes in with a ridiculous valuation."
~ *Kevin Harrington*

The people or organizations who invest financially in entrepreneurial businesses primarily for stock or equity are known as angel investors or venture capitalists; those who provide loans are known as lenders or banks. These investors and capital sources are at times necessary to start or grow a business, though ironically many entrepreneurs consider securing investment an absolute requirement and the "Holy Grail" for achieving early success. Entrepreneurs forget that they are trading upfront investment for ownership and future revenues, while ignoring customers who may offer less money but provide investment early on **only** for the businesses' products or services. *(Moreover, without proper training on how to secure investment, the early cash is as likely to destroy the startup as it is to fast-track it to success.)* So this demonstrates that many entrepreneurs simply don't know when to seek investors or capital sources or even how to connect with them. Likewise, investors want equitable deals and banks only desire and target the businesses that can, or are

"Investment can be extremely valuable for entrepreneurs, or it can be very detrimental! In either scenario the process of finding and securing capital is often long and even expensive. Having a mechanism to match entrepreneurs and investors together is very valuable to both audiences in terms of time and keeping the entrepreneur focused on revenues and growth for their business."

~ *Jo Anne Gabbert*

likely to, repay their debts. So the capital sources are equally as concerned about finding the right company at the right time as entrepreneurs are about securing capital.

Similarly this can be a significant struggle for governments and civic leaders who don't know many capital sources or entre- preneurs seeking investment, and even when they do they rarely know the right time to make the connection. A common fear is that a connection will successfully result in an investment but the business will fail or be unable to repay a debt causing the government or civic leaders to lose credibility. This fear often results in a tight hold on any capital connections and causes leaders to put a hold on introducing an entrepreneur until they are absolutely certain the business will not fail. Unfortunately, this can never be known at the outset.

For example, in Kansas City there are three major angel investor networks: Mid-America Angels, Show-Me Angels, and Women's Capital Connections. In each of the last three years the average number of investments made by the first was roughly seven, while the Women's Capital Connection made significantly more as they have seemingly overcome this chal- lenge. This seems impressive until these 50 investments are ref- erenced against the 3,000 new entrepreneurial ventures starting each month, according to the Kauffman Foundation's Index of Entrepreneurial Activity. So only a fraction of a percent of the startup businesses, or growing businesses for that matter, ever receive investment. This demonstrates that most businesses are struggling to secure an investment that is significantly less likely than the small investments from secured from paid custom- ers. *(Granted, bank loans weren't referenced. These loans have rarely been available to startups since the Great Recession!)*

To gain perspective, a capitalization and early stage investment expert in Kansas City, Josh Leonard, shared with me that when investing he seeks a very specific type of business and entrepreneurial team. His investment depends on a clear understanding of the stages of the business's finances, operations, and market opportunities. Josh added that entrepreneurs will often say anything to secure an investment when pitching their business...so gaining a clear understanding of the stage of business, how it was built, and background about the entrepreneur is difficult at best. Interestingly investors within each of the three investor networks shared similar perspectives. This is in part why Josh and the investor networks each conduct research on an entrepreneur's business before making any investments, called "due diligence". This research represents a "snapshot", when the real need is to show an ongoing record of the business from idea to the present including strategies and actions, much like a "movie". The idea of an ongoing report is incredibly appealing to investors, as most invest in the person and not the idea, and seeing the entrepreneur in action could greatly increase their desire to invest. This insight proves investors and capital sources are seeking more methodical ways to evaluate potential investment opportunities...which may lead to more investments being made.

These investor networks are populated by accredited angel investors, who are verified by the government to have made over $200,000 in the last two years or have a net worth of over $1,000,000. In each community there are also many friends, family, or professionals that will not meet accreditation but still be interested in investing with entrepreneurial ventures in their city or region. These professionals are middle-level white-collar or blue-collar workers who find investing in a business exciting and engaging by being involved at the senior level. Though these investors typically invest only $1,000 to $25,000 in a business, this is often the amount that most startups and some growing businesses require. So while the non-accredited angels will not gain tax credits...they are vital to infusing capital into a community's businesses.

Banks and lending institutions are also a possible source of capital for startups or growing businesses. The critical piece missing in all of this is to understand what the investors and capital sources are looking for, so that they can be effectively paired with an appropriate entrepreneurial venture. This is operation can be driven by the coordinator team, but only if there is a process for identifying what both sides are seeking before facilitating the match.

Hence critical set of requirements were depicted that would need to be identified by each Investor or Capital Source to effectively match them to appropriate entrepreneur opportunities. These requirements should create a profile, identifying:

- Preferred Business Type or Industry
- Preferred Business Age and Revenues
- Preferred Entrepreneur Skill Sets and Background
- Size of Investment (per deal and amount planned per year)
- Desired Way to be Contacted

This profile provides clarity to government and civic leaders on their capital sources, and identifies what each considers to be a good investment.

Dozens of entrepreneurs seek connectivity to investors and capital sources and are constantly frustrated when funding sources which are difficult to track down simply reply that the business is not a good fit for them at this time. This is demoralizing for entrepreneurs and quickly chips away their confidence in their business, which otherwise may be a viable business or idea. To fix this connectivity gap, the investment requirements were aligned within and along the two Guided, Experiential Learning paths. Doing so showcases what investors expect from entrepreneurs and their businesses and the steps to take to prepare for investors. Coaches can be briefed on what investors are seeking so as to help prepare the entrepreneur for pitching to an investor. When an entrepreneur has completed the necessary stages in their path, their coach can nominate them to be matched to investors. At this point, the coach should be confident the entrepreneur has been trained and is prepared to meet with capital sources. To this point and after some discussion with the Advisory Experts, it was suggested that coaches, not entrepreneurs, should complete a similar profile about their client's business to provide a third-party review of the investment opportunity.

"Seasoned Investors prefer to have an "A" team with a "B" idea, rather than an "A" idea with a "B" team. Thus, a motivated entrepreneur with a strong support structure is much more attractive than simply having the most innovative ideas. Government and Civic Leaders create this structure as a competitive advantage to support entrepreneurs!"

~Michie P. Slaughter

Ideally the profile should detail:

- Business Type and Industry
- Business Age and Revenues

- Entrepreneur Skills Sets and Background
- Size of Investment being Sought

By having profiles on investors and entrepreneurs, the coordinator team should be able to compare profiles to identify suitable matches at any given time. Matches can be determined by the coordinator team, to relieve the fear or pressure of a bad introduction, or can be made by government and civic leaders. Doing so helps the investors and capital sources understand their matches are determined through a process which pre-screens entrepreneurs to make them better candidates for securing investment. *(Additionally this allows the entrepreneur to remain focused on customer acquisition, development, and growth, while the coach utilizes the Organic Environment to seek out suitable investors or capital sources.)*

The Investors and Capital Sources Operation is designed to provide clarity and automation to the process of identifying a community of investors and matching them to entrepreneurial businesses seeking capital. This design allows government and civic leaders to orchestrate the connection of entrepreneurs with investors and capital sources without getting directly involved in the transactions or introductions. In Kansas City this approach led to many investments in entrepreneurial businesses and attracted many more inves-

"The unique way of pairing entrepreneurs with investors and capital sources utilizes the many strengths of the professionals in a community and solves many of the connectivity challenges. Utilizing coaches and coordinators to screen the entrepreneurs, find investors, and achieve the match maximizes value and limits the financial expenses of the community's Organic Environment or ecosystem."

~ Danny Lobina

tors and entrepreneurs due to the ease of connectivity and the pre-screened introductions. This generated strong investment opportunities, business growth, and economic outcomes for the community. The Investors and Capital Sources Operation fits into the Entrepreneur Operational Infrastructure as depicted in the diagram.

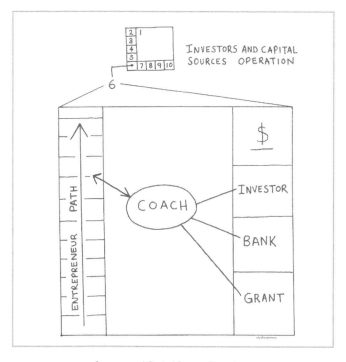

Investors and Capitol Sources Operations

Operation 7: Experiential Events

"Experience: that most brutal of teachers. But you learn, my God do you learn." ~ C.S. Lewis

The path to start or grow a business is extremely difficult and often feels like sprinting a marathon. Entrepreneurs are constantly working to develop their businesses to achieve the next milestone and to search for advice or new customers along the way. Events provide rare opportunities for entrepreneurs to connect with many people from the community at one time to gain advice and potential customers. Events generate opportunities for a community to collaborate with entrepreneurs, spotlight their businesses, and recognize the many people that are supporting business owners and their economy...specifically the mentors, coaches, investors and capital sources, coordinator teams, and other leaders involved with the community-branded, Organic Environment. Thus events are incredibly rewarding and valuable for entrepreneurs and for the community.

Events powerfully showcase the pure energy generated from starting or growing businesses to the community, building entrepreneurial momentum in the city or region. The challenge for events is that the powerful experience only lasts for two to three hours and then the energy dissipates. An even greater challenge is how to transmit the event experience beyond the walls of the venue, so that everyone in the community can gain value and insights even if they are not in attendance. For example, early on in my entrepreneur career I was a partner in DigiRace, a startup tracking company for auto-racing. This business was chosen to pitch at the investment forum called Invest Midwest. The benefit to DigiRace was the opportunity to pitch our investment opportunity in front of an auditorium of investors. Afterwards however, many in the community were unaware of the event or its importance to the city's or region's businesses because they had not experienced Invest Midwest. It may seem obvious that by not attending a person would miss the experience, but to empower the community to embrace entrepreneurship it is important that the masses remotely gain the experience. Most people aren't able to attend NFL football games, but they understand the value, experience, and outcomes of every game because of the media. So it is important for entrepreneurial events to broadcast their results in order to achieve that same level of engagement.

Events can be a powerful tool to encourage a community to care and embrace entrepreneurship, but to accomplish this they must understand each entrepreneur being showcased and gain an appreciation for the work necessary for selection. Failing to do this creates a "context gap" for the community. Think about the last time you heard about the winner of a sporting event that you have rarely heard of, like Cricket in the U.S. or American Football elsewhere in the world. Obviously, the winner did something right to beat out the competition, but without an appreciation for the sport or the personal stories of the winners...significance is lost. Thus for a community to truly appreciate, support, and rally behind entrepreneurs they must understand the context, which requires communication of these three steps:

1. The number of entrepreneurs applying to the event and the process for being selected.

2. The work, in the form of a story, that each entrepre-

neur took to reach the event.

3. The struggles and successes of each entrepreneur to reach the event.

"Entrepreneurial events in general are very beneficial to entrepreneurs for their feedback and provide the community an opportunity to learn about local businesses. Experiential events increase in value by interweaving the participants and audience into a program that supersedes the 3-hour event. Further the experience creates a perception of ongoing momentum that is exciting and very contagious!"

~ Barry J Crocker

It is easy to understand how this tells a story and creates an experience that can generate a sense of excitement and context for each event. *(This approach is used in Olympic broadcasts, which depict the stories of each athlete and their struggles to reach the games.)* The attending audience and community will gain a greater appreciation for the paths, Organic Environment, and nine entrepreneurial operations supporting entrepreneurs. Just think how much more support could be gained for entrepreneurship by dramatizing the economic benefits of each business that is operating in the city or region, as depicted through the event. Positioning events in this way creates an experience that starts before the day of the event and can last well beyond the next entrepreneurial happening. This positioning also inspires, motivates, and engages the community to support entrepreneurship as a strategy to grow the city's or region's economy!

To achieve this, the corresponding coordinator team and government and civic leaders should host at least one experiential event each quarter, specifically focusing on one of these three entrepreneur community focuses: Startup, Growing Business, or Entrepreneur-Investor Pitch. The overviews for each of the three event focuses, are:

Startup Experiential Event
(known as startFEST+DEMO)

This experiential event showcases select startup businesses in a city or region, providing the community an opportunity to meet and collaborate with the entrepreneurs they have been learning about from the coordinator team's communications. The goal of the startup experiential event is to showcase entrepreneurs in the city's or region's branded Organic Environment's StartPath, as well as their coaches, mentors, resource vendors, secured investors or capital sources, and coordinator teams, helping to transform ideas into revenue-generating businesses.

BoostLeesSummit's Organic Environment launched its first startFEST+DEMO in the first 3 months of operation with a crowd of more than 150 people who were in awe of the nine startups incubating in the city of Lee's Summit, Missouri, unbenounced to them. Mark Dickey, an administrator of Boost Lee's Summit, truly gained a greater appreciation for their branded Organic Environment after watching how the community's interactions with startups increased their excitement for supporting entrepreneurship. Mark is a believer in startup demo events and believes the community's attendance creates an experiential realization for the value of fostering entrepreneurship!

Growth Business Experiential Event
(known as GrowFEST)

This experiential event showcases the types of entrepreneurial businesses thriving in the city or region. It provides the community a chance to meet and collaborate with some of the entrepreneurs they have been learning about from the coordinator teams' communications. The goal of the growing business experiential event is to showcase entrepreneurs participating within GrowPath in the community's branded, Organic Environment. In addition to showcasing the growing businesses, the event offers the opportunity to promote their coaches, mentors, resource vendors, investors and capital sources, and the coordinator teams helping to transform existing business in the community into growing corporations.

Contributing Author and Partner of Evis Consulting and StartKC, Barry Crocker helped launch the first GrowFEST. The event was designed to experientially showcase growing businesses to the audience from the community as a way to expand the perceived business activity happening in the city or region and to reward those entrepreneurs utilizing the GrowPath. Barry foresaw that innovative experiential events were often focused solely on startups, and expressed the need to extend this experience to growing businesses, who are often the drivers of a city's or region's economy...especially in rural regions. Barry's expressed perspectives and support gave six businesses the opportunity to present to an attending audience of over 200 investors, business owners, executives, and others from the community. Feedback from the event was incredibly strong as entrepreneurs were given a unique opportunity to present their businesses, and then later demonstrate their products and services to potential customers, investors, and strategic partners. GrowFEST was an experience that not only helped the six presenting businesses, but also inspired other businesses to focus more on growth and to get involved with their Organic Environment.

Entrepreneur-Investor Pitch Experiential Event
(known as PitchON!)

This experiential pitch event showcases the investors and capital sources available in a city or region, live demonstrations for how to successfully pitch, and promotes an elite line up of starting and growing entrepreneurs. Since most entrepreneurs seeking capital are unaware of how to pitch or how to gain access to these sources, the event creates a perfect marketing opportunity for the branded Organic Environment to attract entrepreneurs by demonstrating the streamlined process. Additionally this event appeals to angel investors and other capital sources as an opportunity to leverage the community's branded Organic Environment and gain better startup or growth-based business deal flow. It also provides the community the self-realization that the capital, entrepreneurs, and structure *(through the coordinator teams)* are readily available to grow the city's or region's economy from within! The focused goal for the entrepreneur-investor pitch event is to showcase the startup and growth-focused entrepreneurs and investors that are engaging to increase business outcomes and, ultimately, economic results. The events additionally promote the coordinator teams, coaches, mentors, and resource vendors supporting the entrepreneurs and their businesses on a daily basis.

The GrowMidMo Organic Environment held a PitchON! to showcase the entrepreneurs and investors that were operating and thriving in their region. As GrowMidMo operates across four rural counties, the event provided these communities a chance to experience the grassroots businesses that were operating in their region. Danny Lobina, a co-Administrator of GrowMidMo and Director of the region's SBTDC, shared that many in the community were shocked by the innovative businesses and upcoming entrepreneurs that were developing in the region, and inspired by the many local investors that were focused on providing capital to the region's businesses. Danny believes that the entrepreneurs and investors gained strong value from the meetings and believes that this started a chain reaction that will benefit many entrepreneurs in the future, as well as attract many investors to join their Organic Environment. Danny is even more excited by the draw the event had in motivating the community to offer greater support to the area's businesses, and attracting aspiring entrepreneurs off the sidelines and onto the paths to make their vision a reality for themselves and their community!

Each event creates a unique experience designed to increase the momentum and activity within the community. The reason for always promoting those involved is to constantly nurture the perception of activities and economic growth from within the city or region, but also to help aspiring entrepreneurs or businesses on the sidelines realize how to imitate the success of those being showcased at the event. Experiential events really are an essential part of the entire Organic Environment methodology.

While the three experiential events focuses have been found to provide strong value to entrepreneurs and the community, there are many more focuses and types of events that can utilize the "3-step experiential event process" to more effectively provide education, training, or networking opportunities. These events are very valuable and can be placed throughout the Guided, Experiential Learning paths to attract greater entrepreneur and Community Audiences to attend. Positioning these additional events in the paths will allow entrepreneurs to self-realize the need for the event, and utilize the

"There is no greater excitement and inspiration for entrepreneurs than to witness fellow entrepreneurs succeeding. Experiential events bottle that excitement because the entrepreneurs and investors on display encourage others to get involved. Further, experiential events provide the community confidence that local and regional entrepreneurs can grow their economy, and by becoming a business owner it is possible to achieve one's own dreams!"

~ Barry J Crocker

coaches to reinforce the value to be gained.

The Experiential Events Operation greatly enhances entrepreneurs' abilities to gain broad community perspectives and support for their startups and growing businesses. Experiential events support the community coordinators' efforts to promote and communicate how entrepreneurs are improving a city's or region's economy. The Experiential Events Operation will exponentially enhance the community's awareness of entrepreneurship, mobilize big shifts in the culture, and create a promotion incentive for entrepreneurs as they work through the paths. The Experiential Events Operation fits within the Entrepreneur Operational Infrastructure as described in the diagram.

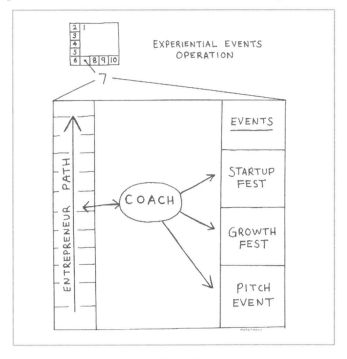

Experiental Events Operation

Operation 8: Media and Promotion

*"Without promotion, something terrible happens…
nothing!" ~ P.T. Barnum*

The Media and Promotion Operation is critical in generating awareness within the community for their many local entrepreneurial businesses. It is also critical to many entrepreneurs' success for them to experience early support and attract early revenues from the community. This is primarily achieved when the coordinator teams identify new and growing businesses and promote their accomplishments and value through the mainstream media, social media, and word of mouth. The intent is that Comfluencers and Efluencers in the city or region will resonate with these developments and further advocate for entrepreneurship in the community. This approach also provides early support for the entrepreneurs and provides assurance that the community is looking out for their business interests.

The media attention tells entrepreneurs that their involvement and progress in the community's

"Using media to promote new and growing businesses in a community builds awareness for partnerships and customers. The community's efforts to use Media and Promotion for their entrepreneurs strengthens the businesses and demonstrates the community's support. Further, a community's perception of the entrepreneur community and its impact on the economy is often directly related to what the city or region's masses are made aware of. So promoting entrepreneurs not only helps the businesses but also helps the community to mutually grow."

~ Barry J Crocker

branded Organic Environment *(specifically utilizing StartPath or GrowPath, coaches, and mentors)* is likely to generate promotion and recognition for their business. It is a strong motivator and driver to encourage continued enrollment and use of this grassroots effort. Without an interconnected infrastructure to document business developments and growth, the approach for coordinators to identify or promote the entrepreneurial activities in their region is not clear. This leaves entrepreneurs with the sole responsibility of promoting their business to the community. The "interconnected organic approach" to promotion requires entrepreneurs to utilize the available operations to support the start or growth of their business, and by doing so grants them the benefits of being connected and promoted by their community through its branded Organic Environment.

While promotion of a business can be very good, it is also very important to limit the types of information promoted about the entrepreneur. This can be achieved in the paths by having the entrepreneur and coach select the information they desire to have shared, assuring them both that any confidential information discussed will not be promoted.

This challenge was faced and addressed early on by Danny Lobina, an administrator with GrowMidMo and the Director of the Small Business Technology Development Center at Moberly Area Community College. Danny realized the value to entrepreneurs of promoting their businesses, but was also conscious to not cause damage by promoting the wrong information. So Danny suggested that coaches be utilized to help entrepreneurs screen the information that could be promoted to the community.

The Media and Promotion Operation provides entrepreneurs the confidence to know their community wants to be supportive and is ready to promote their progress and successes. The Media and Promotion Operation fits within the Entrepreneur Operational Infrastructure as detailed in the diagram.

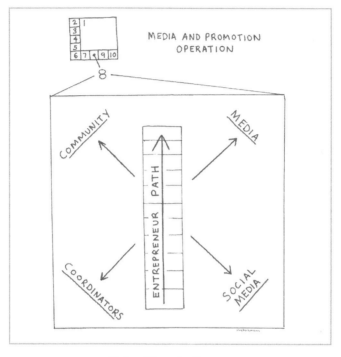

Media and Promotion Operation

Operation 9: Community Development

"Action is the Foundational Key to All Success."
~ Pablo Picasso

In 2010, I had the pleasure to work with a mead wine entrepreneur named Susan Liebhart. Her company, Pantera Mead, used honey to make a form of alcohol similar to sweet wine, which was absolutely delicious. Like many entrepreneurs, Susan was passionate about her mead and had made an assortment of flavors and even found a strong customer base at Renaissance Festivals. Her struggle was translating that one-weekend-a-year audience into a repeat customer base in Blue Springs, MO, a suburb of Kansas City. Essentially, Susan's need came down to campaigning for the community to buy her mead. Having the coordinator team and Comfluencers promote her local business and advocate for the community to be patrons, helped Susan and built to the city's or region's economy.

"Fostering support for entrepreneurship is critical but difficult for cities and regions, especially when the community isn't currently established. So having coordinators to engage the community as "ambassadors" to influence support is priceless! This grassroots approach to community development is likely to go viral and quickly build a very strong and notable entrepreneur community, greatly aiding the efforts of leaders!"

~ Dr. Bernard Franklin

Now let's be clear, this does not mean that the community development coordinator team and Comfluencers should spam every household to buy the products and services of every business in the Organic Environment. It does mean advocating to the community the products and services of a select few start-ups or growing businesses that can strengthen and accelerate the economy. Doing this will create a buzz around the city or region, and the community will begin to actively look and seek out these startups and growing businesses. Unless you call the community's attention to these businesses, they will unintentionally overlook them. *(If you want to test this theory, check out how many cars are white the next time you drive You may not have realized quite how many there are, until you are purposefully looking for them.)*

The value of community development for entrepreneurs is to create an awareness and support for their new or growing business from the community. This will allow entrepreneurs to stay focused on building their businesses, expedite the attraction of customers, and gain customer feedback to quickly make improvements to better their offerings. This "feedback loop" is strongly advocated in the *Lean Startup*, by Eric Ries. By pulling the community to the entrepreneur, it requires less time for the business owner to find potential customers and more time to refine their product or service to meet the needs of the customer. This may seem like a marginal gain, but an entrepreneur in that turbulent cycle gains a 'breath of fresh air' when the community works with them to grow their business.

So the Community Development Operation is the active engagement of the community around new and growing entrepreneurial businesses through word of mouth promotion and relationship building. The coordinator team and Comfluencers organically engaged must remember the Community and Entrepreneur Social Infrastructures to ensure a positive response. The Community Development Operation fits into the Entrepreneur Operational Infrastructure as described in the diagram.

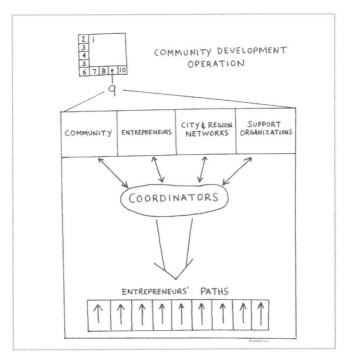

Community Development Operation

Operation 10: Metrics

"The real metric of success isn't the size of your bank account. It's the number of lives in whom you might be able to make a positive difference." ~ Naveen Jain

Tracking and measuring entrepreneurs progress is critically important. The paths and other operations in the Entrepreneur Operational Infrastructure offer multiple measuring points to track entrepreneurs and the Community Audiences working in the community-branded Organic Environment. This provides government and civic leaders, the community, and coordinator teams the insights to identify how entrepreneurs are succeeding and failing in their city or region. They can then allot additional resources and time to areas of weakness in supporting entrepreneurs, their businesses, and the many support programs and vendors.

"Measures and metrics of entrepreneurial success and failures are critical for a community to be supportive of entrepreneurship. Getting high marks in launching and growing successful businesses will attract others who want to be surrounded by a community that supports entrepreneurial success."

~ Jo Anne Gabbert

Reporting the metrics of fellow entrepreneurs in similar industries or types of businesses helps entrepreneurs set expectations as to the amount of time and money it will take to start or grow their business. This provides psychological motivation to entrepreneurs when they are struggling in critical stages of their business, knowing that many other entrepreneurs have faced similar struggles.

Finally, business results can be translated into data-based metrics that can benefit the many resource vendors, investors and capital sources, mentors, coaches, and other support programs by providing statistical business outcomes that were affected by the support, investments, and services provided to entrepreneurs. It can also depict how increased investments of time and money into the community-led Organic Environment's infrastructures and operations could achieve even greater returns for entrepreneurs, the many support audiences, the community, and most importantly the city's or region's economy!

"Tracking entrepreneurial businesses is incredibly difficult and time-consuming. Systematically gathering information provides a city or region the ability to trend entrepreneurial business and identify areas requiring increased support. Ultimately, the better the tracking the better the decisions that can be made."

~ Christopher Doroh

Seeing individual and communal results is incredibly important, as it demonstrates to all involved that this infrastructure is valuable to all audiences and is worth continued investment. If you think about the many metrics that could be tracked throughout the paths *(i.e. how long it takes to progress through topics, achievements in each topic, and growth of business)* or through resource vendors *(i.e. measuring the type of services provided and the business outcomes of those services)*, as well as the many other Organic Environment's operations that could be tracked, it is incredible. Furthermore the value of what could be better managed, better understood, and better facilitated to help entrepreneurs build their businesses bigger and faster...is insurmountable. In fact, as we showcased these results and metrics to Jeff Kaczmarek in Kansas City, he told us that this was the type of information that could guide investments into entrepreneurship, as it answered the many questions for how dollars invested in entrepreneurship created jobs from multiple levels of engagement. Thus the metrics from across the Entrepreneur Operational Infrastructure are invaluable for government and civic leaders to clearly view the entrepreneurial and business situation and how to pinpoint strategies that increase economic outputs.

The Metrics operation becomes incredibly valuable for measuring the effectiveness of each operation in the Entrepreneur Operational Infrastructure and the productivity of supporting entrepreneurs in starting and growing their businesses. While the metrics that can be measured and researched are vast, tracking entrepreneurs' startup and growth progressions generates the necessary information needed to organically manage and build a city's or region's economy, both now and into the future. The Metrics Operation fits into the Entrepreneur Operational Infrastructure as depicted in the diagram.

"Entrepreneurial Metrics provide leaders with the insights to measure business creation and growth across a city or region. Measuring the effectiveness and outcomes of entrepreneurship in a program is pretty standard, but doing it across an entire city or region's programs was all but impossible until now. This ability provides a whole new level of measurement and allows leaders greater insights into how to generate new jobs and grow the entire economic environment."

~ Lisa Franklin

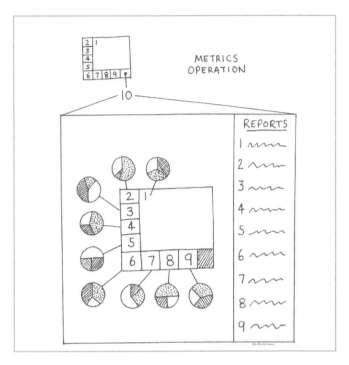

Metrics Operation

Entrepreneur Operational Infrastructure Review

The Entrepreneur Operational Infrastructure provides a guide to integrate and network together the operations needed to support entrepreneurs who are starting or growing businesses. Doing so will significantly increase the benefit to entrepreneurs by decreasing the time needed to achieve a revenue-generating business or greater revenue outputs. Additionally this networking guide will leverage the coordinator teams to promote businesses and their development to the community, thereby increasing the awareness and potential for interactions with the city's or region's entrepreneurs. These two outcomes will quickly and organically evolve community motivation and drive to support entrepreneurship and grow the economy... thereby increasing the livelihood of everyone in the community.

(Note: The Entrepreneur Operational Infrastructure has made multiple recommendations on using specific tools and website portals when forming the Organic Environment. These tools and portals will need to be built and designed to achieve the Organic Environment in the suggested 18 - 24 months, a process that can take years to achieve. There is an Organic Environment template that contains a manual, tools, and website portals that can be customized to any city or region, which can be purchased through www.EvisThrive. com. Along with these templates, Advisory Experts insights and recommendations can be secured to further accelerate and grow your city's or region's economy.)

So the Entrepreneur Operational Infrastructure acts as the proverbial "GPS" that guides entrepreneurs through the journey of starting or growing businesses, and is the mechanism that connects the business owners to the support programs and resources at the moment they realize a need. This proverbial "GPS" also aids government and civic leaders and the coordinator teams to understand how the networked, Organic Environment can start and grow the desired types of industries and businesses in their city or region. In effect, this mechanism provides clarity to understand and gain the tools necessary to purposefully stabilize and grow an economy. Each of the 10 operations fit within the Entrepreneur Operational Infrastructure as depicted in the diagram.

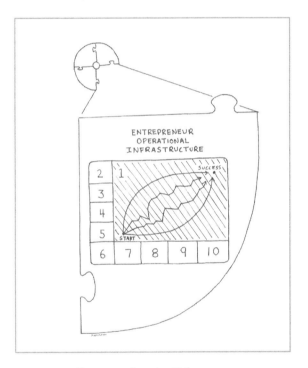

Entrepreneur Operational Infrastructure

"Interconnecting the entrepreneurial support operations and programs in a city or region enhances the benefit of each. This allows entrepreneurs to focus more time on building their business while utilizing proven strategies, and leveraging the communities existing programs to connect the resources needed 'Just-in-Time.' This supports entrepreneurs at a level rarely duplicated outside Silicon Valley!"

~ *Dr. Bernard Franklin*

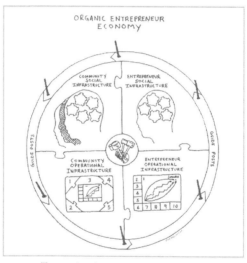

The complete *Organic Entrepreneur Economy*:
Organic Environment, four Infrastructures and 6 Guideposts

Chapter 9:

The Organic Environment Guideposts

The four community and entrepreneur infrastructures depict how to develop a supportive community and foster entrepreneurship activity. The simple realities behind *The Organic Entrepreneur Economy* are: 1) Focus on understanding the entrepreneurs and community, and 2) Focus on the operational and strategic solutions. The successful evolution of entrepreneurship, the community and its culture, and the economy are all dependent on these two focal points. The entrepreneurs' and communities' perception is their interpretation of the environment combined with their mindsets, and the result is social norms, or the customary rules that govern behavior in groups or societies. *(According to the Stanford*

"To successfully foster entrepreneurship and grow the economy requires understanding the motivations of everyone involved and providing a framework that allows everyone to achieve their goals. The two simple realities: 1) understanding and 2) solutions, are critical to achieving the outcomes discussed in The Organic Entrepreneur Economy. Without both, growth just isn't feasible."

~ Mark W. Dickey

Encyclopedia of Philosophy) Understanding these "customary rules" helps the community to organically accelerate the evolutionary process for entrepreneurs, the community and its culture, as well as the economy.

> *"Changing the culture, or customary rules, in a community has often been described as nearly impossible and a campaign that requires decades. However, now that the social mindsets and operations have been reviewed through the infrastructures, it is a more defined process with a greater likelihood of success. Once the variables are understood and a plan of action is in place...the only step left is to implement an execution plan."*
>
> ~ Dr. Bernard Franklin

This reality was proven on a spectacular scale during the Great Recession when publicly traded companies had stock prices below their cash on hand. If you bought all the shares of one of those companies, the price would be less than the amount of money in the corporation's bank account. This absurd valuation occurred when investors perceived that the United States and the corporations therein were no longer financially viable, and these perceptions became the communally adopted social norms, so everyone stopped supporting these investments or sold their stock. Another example pertaining more to entrepreneurship was a perception in the iconic Silicon Valley, where during the Great Recession starting a business continued to be considered safe enough for parents to encourage their kids to become entrepreneurs. These parents' perception of entrepreneurship as being a beneficial career option was reinforced by other parents who supported that social view. Thus the perception and actions of these parents became the cultural and social norm.

The focused 2-step process guiding the Organic Environment is:

1. **Focus on Understanding Entrepreneurs and the Community** - Government and civic leaders seek to understand the entrepreneurs' and communities' perceptions and mindsets that result in social norms.

2. **Focus on Operational and Strategic Solutions** - Government and civic leaders utilize their understanding to empower the community to interconnect operations and strategies that support entrepreneurs.

This process accelerates the organic evolution of the cultural and social norms, generates community support, and fosters entrepreneurship, which stabilizes and grows the economy.

While the four Infrastructures provide the architecture for organic acceleration, the guidance to apply and implement the Infrastructures is found within six Guideposts:

1. Remember

2. Position

3. Attract

4. Generate

5. Monitor

6. Empower! Empower! Empower!

"These two steps are so important to truly achieve immediate and lasting entrepreneurial, community and economic growth. As seen throughout history, change is best accomplished when the target audiences and their culture are first understood and then offered a better "mousetrap." This approach ensures that as the entrepreneur and community populations evolve, government and civic leaders can continue to set expectations and meet their needs."

~ Barry J Crocker

"Facilitating the Organic Environment and Infrastructures according to the Guideposts is essential, as it ensures accelerated success! This observation comes directly from my experiences with GrowBlueSprings. I helped to build the Guideposts, and as a result I have witnessed the fast-paced benefits that have ensued!"

~ Brien M. Starner

The Guideposts have been proven to help government and civic leaders successfully apply the Organic Environment and Infrastructures to their city or region and to accelerate the achievement of results to just 18 - 24 months...as opposed to decades.

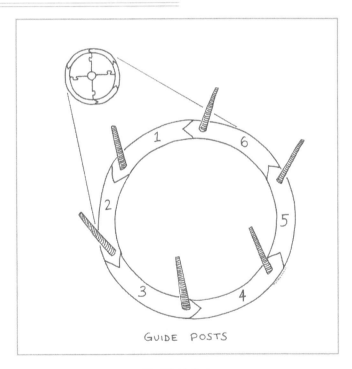

GUIDE POSTS

The 6 Guide Posts

Guidepost 1: Remember

"A people without the knowledge of their past history, origin and culture is like a tree without roots."
~ Marcus Garvey

In the past, cities and regions struggling to foster business creation and growth were almost always founded on the backs of entrepreneurs. The purpose of people gathering or grouping together in cities or regions was to exchange goods and services, as well as to increase their economic potential as a whole. So entrepreneurship was a significant part of every city's or region's history and is still included in their culture, or DNA. Leaders and others in the community need to remember how their businesses were originally fostered. Remembering and embracing these past entrepreneurial roots is often difficult, but extremely important, as it will jumpstart the community much faster than trying to recreate its existence. Even though entrepreneurship is often a slightly foreign approach for government and civic leaders, there are many people in a community who have small business ownership in their heritage. These people are very knowledgeable and passionate about returning their city or region to an entrepreneurial state which can stabilize and grow the economy through

"Economies are built over time by many entrepreneurs, and remembering those who played vital roles in building a city or region's economy is important. As the descendants of those entrepreneurs, many with substantial influence and money can become strong proponents of entrepreneurship and a community's Organic Environment."

~ Steve Meinzen

small business ownership.

It is likely that many of the businesses and corporations in a city or region are currently led by entrepreneurs, or their descendants, and are deeply rooted in and driven to improve the community. These entrepreneurs and their descendants are often the Comfluencers who will influence community support of the branded Organic Environment. So remembering to provide these Comfluencers a seat at the table and recognizing their historical and current entrepreneurial contributions will rally others in the community to join the cause. In an effort to move forward, a focus must be put on remembering past entrepreneurs and their successes and embracing their and their descendants' perspective and influence.

"A successful grassroots effort requires collaboration and community-wide support to be successful. A big part of this includes embracing the older, successful generations that are idolized by many throughout the community. To gain their support and influence, they must see how valued their involvement is and how their past achievements are important to future successes in the community."

~ Barry J Crocker

In Kansas City, it was no different. To gain support and resources for the branded Organic Environment, coined StartKC, an early focus and credit was given to the many entrepreneurial businesses and organizations that helped shape the current economy. One of these was Danny O'Neill, founder of The Roasterie (a producer or premium gourmet coffee) and the Entrepreneurial Exchange (a group for the entrepreneurial founders from some of the most entrepreneurial and successful corporations in Kansas City). Providing this early credit as we worked to implement the four infrastructures helped to gain valuable perspectives, generate much needed early support, and even attract some financial resources for hosting events and promoting the community-led StartKC.

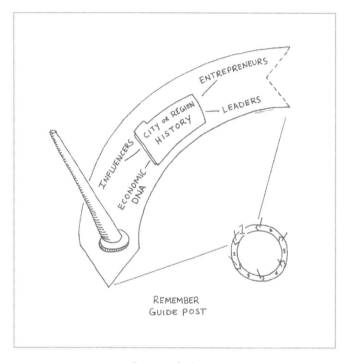

Remember Guidepost

Guidepost 2: Position

"While we can remember the past, we cannot write the future. Only our children, the future of our community, can do that." ~ Jonathan Sacks

Any city or region that seeks to foster a strong entrepreneurial environment with a supportive culture must secure a strong commitment from the Community Audiences *(specifically Comfluencers, Efluencers, and Doers)* and coordinator teams. This "Commitment Base" does not grant the government or civic leadership any ownership or power over the base or Organic Environment, but rather legitimizes the grassroots effort to prevent it from being mistakenly overlapped by other political or interest-based organizations. This commitment base can also promote the perception to the communal masses that the Organic Environment really is a grassroots effort to improve the city's or region's economy. The commitment base's position will be evident when the Organic Environment and infrastructures are launched, when the coordinators are actively communicating progress, and when entrepreneurial success is seen in the community. This will in turn entice more involvement in the community's grassroots effort and attract new and growing entrepreneurs to engage.

"Embracing the community early and offering support from the sidelines is critical if the community is to feel empowered and driven to achieve success. This has been our approach with Grow Mid-Missouri, which has been very effective."

~ Corey J. Mehaffy

For StartKC, Kansas City's branded Organic Environment,

there were informal connections made with the Chamber of Commerce and Economic Development Corporation. These involvements along with the strong support of many entrepreneurial companies created a strong presence for the grassroots effort. Having this commitment base in place allowed the bootstrapped StartKC to quickly launch a suite of entrepreneur events *(adding GrowFEST and PitchON to the existing startFEST)* that attracted hundreds of entrepreneur and community attendees within 12 months. The commitment base created a groundswell of additional support from the community and entrepreneurs to further support entrepreneurs through StartKC. Additional entrepreneurial programs and services were launched, through the empowerment operation and perception that entrepreneurship was gaining momentum. The momentum lured government and civic organizations to rush in and support the perceived base of new and growing entrepreneurs.

> *"If government, civic, or corporate leaders try to control the tempo or pace of entrepreneurship in their city or region, they will not succeed. Instead, entrepreneurs will simply "move the meeting" somewhere else. Government, civic and corporate leaders should invite entrepreneurs to participate on important community boards as a way to encourage and support the pace of entrepreneurship in their community."*
>
> ~ Jo Anne Gabbert

At this point the excitement of entrepreneurial activity caused government and civic organizations to rush in and rival StartKC with additional support programs. This instantly began to cannibalize the grassroots effort and StartKC. For this reason, it is essential to have a formal relationship with a sponsoring government or civic organization to ensure that their help is effectively managed to benefit entrepreneurs and add momentum to any existing programs. Lessons and insights learned by StartKC should be shared with the incoming government and civic organizations, helping the entire city's and region's programs, organizations, and Organic Environment to work together to grow the momentum and maximize economic outcomes!

Since Kansas City, the Advisory Experts and social entrepreneurs from Evis Consulting have had the opportunity to revise and re-facilitate the commitment base as has been suggested, and the results have been better than imagined. Over time, as lessons are shared and momentum is gained by cities that share a region, the regional community's sense of ownership grows and forms partnerships that significantly accelerate the economic momentum and collective outcomes. In fact, Jackson County, Missouri *(which is the county for Kansas City, Missouri and several eastern suburbs)* embraced the Organic Environment after viewing the effects within three of its cities: Kansas City, Blue Springs, and Lee's Summit. Thus Jackson County was able to learn how to be complementary in their involvements and sponsored the creation of a countywide showcase

> *"While StartKC was not one of the Economic Development Corporation's initiatives, I saw it more as an approach to support the community. I realized early on that my organization's involvement needed to be from an influence and support role to allow the community to perceive ownership and free will, even though having greater connectivity to the program may have yielded more benefits."*
>
> *~ Jeff Kaczmarek*

event for the retailers. This grew the existing momentum in all three cities. Jackson County's Economic Development Executive, Robbie Makinen, identified ways to utilize the communities in each suburb to embrace the event so that it worked within the existing infrastructures, thereby showcasing entrepreneurs that had been screened and prepped for the event. This is just one of the many examples for how the commitment base has positioned involvements to achieve even greater outcomes.

It is critical, when facilitating the branded Organic Environment, that a government or civic organization be positioned to support the community-led grassroots effort.

"Designing and facilitating the Organic Environment has been a very successful and rewarding process, accompanied by many learning experiences along the way. We transitioned from early to sustained growth during StartKC. The Advisory Experts and I were able to improve the Organic Environment from this experience. These improvements will occur in any community facilitating an ecosystem. For leaders, it would be beneficial and safest to focus on an ecosystem that has had the most success and improvements. That is the determinant of success - succeeding in the market consistently."

~ Dr. Bernard Franklin

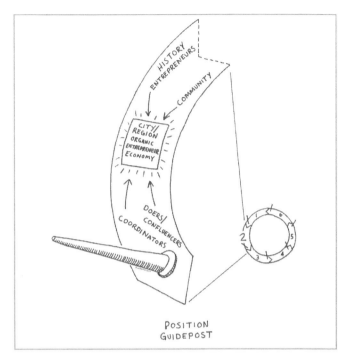

POSITION
GUIDEPOST

Position Guidepost

Guidepost 3: Attract

"Continuing economic growth requires both recruitment of new companies and expansion of existing businesses."
~ Phil Bredesen

Attracting entrepreneurs is the single greatest concern for government and civic leaders who are contemplating the adoption of the Organic Environment or any other entrepreneur ecosystem for their city or region. Enticing entrepreneurs to any environment requires strong financial and time investments, as well as an integrated recruiting mechanism. In the Organic Environment this requirement is operationally built in for each community. Entrepreneurs are a part of the community, which makes it relatively easy for the Community Audiences and coordinator teams to refer the business owners they know to the branded Organic Environment and locate many more through personal and grassroots engagements.

"Attracting entrepreneurs in the Organic Environment is really just an outcome of the process, rather than a constant task. The Organic Environment focuses on using the community to build an organic ecosystem and economy, as opposed to building an entrepreneur program in a city or region first, and then telling the community how to use it."

~ Danny Lobina

The most interesting insight that we garnered from the Organic Environment was that entrepreneurs who learn about programs or services that helped their peers achieve success are intensely drawn to those resources and motivated to supersede them. Cities and regions that are perceived to have a growing number of startup business successes

"The most underutilized approach to recruiting startup or growth entrepreneurs is to promote their peer's successes. For the "if he/she can do it, then I can do it better" mentality will drive many to prove their worth in the region. This will also attract entrepreneurs outside of the community, who will perceive an immersion of entrepreneurial activity and be drawn to the city or region by the perception that their business will have a greater chance of success."

~ Barry J Crocker

"Utilizing this "entrepreneurial mindset" will actually work with growing businesses as well. This approach significantly attracts growing entrepreneurs from outside the region, along with aspiring startup entrepreneurs."

~ Corey J. Mehaffy

can utilize this to attract additional entrepreneurs. Hearing from other entrepreneurs about these successes generates more excitement and energy, which draws in more and more motivated business owners. The beauty of this cause and effect behavior is that it happens organically. As entrepreneurs achieve success in a city or region they instinctively share the news with their friends and fellow entrepreneurs, causing friends and fellow entrepreneurs to effectively engage in the city or region to start or build their business.

The ironic truth behind this behavior is that entrepreneurs almost always believe they are smarter and more capable than their entrepreneurial peers. This little internal drive within every existing or aspiring entrepreneur is a behavioral mechanism that can significantly accelerate the rate of attraction to the Organic Environment and momentum behind the city's or region's economy. *(This behavioral mechanism works for recruiting established and growing businesses as well, aiding government, civic, and economic development leaders in attracting growing businesses to relocate in their city or region.)*

Attracting the entrepreneurial masses to a branded Organic Environment depends on the government and civic leaders correctly implementing the four infrastructures, allowing the coordinator teams to lead the way, and communicating successes to perpetuate the perception that a multitude of businesses are starting and growing in a city or region.

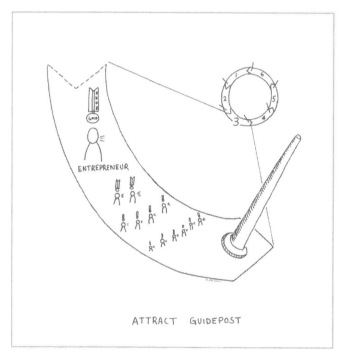

ATTRACT GUIDEPOST

Attract Guidepost

Guidepost 4: Generate

"A goal is a dream with a deadline." ~ Napoleon Hill

As the four infrastructures are implemented within the Organic Environment, entrepreneurial startups and businesses will begin to progress and develop faster than ever before. Coordinator teams will provide support through the ten entrepreneur operations and by communicating the entrepreneurial activity and successes to the community. These coordinator and entrepreneur activities, coupled with communications, will generate excitement and build trust in the community for a stronger economy. The trick with momentum is to sustain and build upon it until the Organic Environment has achieved a critical mass of adoption with entrepreneurs and the community. Only then will the culture evolve enough to stabilize and grow the economy.

"Momentum is the force that fuels a change in culture. To enact change in the community mindsets requires the perception of safety and benefits. Promoting success builds momentum that maximizes the perceived benefits and makes the change seem appealing and safe. This generates and promotes momentum to the community that reinforces the economic and entrepreneurial growth being achieved."

~ Dr. Bernard Franklin

To generate sustainable, growing momentum requires the facilitation of these four strategies:

1. Set Entrepreneur Goals - Think back to the Community Operational Infrastructure in which the types of industries and businesses that are desired in a city or region are chosen. Then together as a community *(mean-*

ing government and civic leaders, coordinators, Community Audiences) goals for attracting these entrepreneurs are decided upon. It is important to focus on concrete business goals like the number of startups, revenue growth for existing businesses, and other goals that can easily be identified when achieved. *(While outcomes are the purpose for setting goals, it is important not to set an outcome as a goal. For instance, it is not easy to determine when the 'create more jobs' outcome has been reached as a goal, as success is likely to be different for different people. So be sure it easy to determine when you have achieved your chosen goals.)*

2. Set Community Goals - Again, think back to the Community Operational Infrastructure and decide the community and cultural outcomes desired. It is important to identify concrete goals like a new incubator, 3 coordinators per operation, $15,000 of sponsorships for events, and other goals that are easy to identify when reached. *(Resist the temptation to set qualitative or social goals, like culture change, as these are difficult to define and even harder to determine when they have been achieved.)*

3. Facilitate an Action Plan *(to reach set goals)* - The Community and Entrepreneur Operational Infrastructures have already prescribed high-level operational plans that need to be achieved. Having a strategic plan *(i.e. when to host events, how often to promote the activity to the community, and when to promote media coverage)* creates a perception of continued activity and momentum. So having a plan that has impending events built-in entices entrepreneurs and Community Audiences to immediately get involved, as well as ensure that target goals are met. These activities perpetuate the perception of momentum!

Set Milestones *(to motivate progress toward goals)* - Milestones are critical in the planning and goal setting process as they provide a measurement or orientation towards accomplishing momentum. This may sound overly obvious, but soon after the Organic Environment and Infrastructures are in place the community and entrepreneurs will be able to identify the improvements. Then a tidal wave of new ideas and new directions will be suggested for the city and region, which will all seem exciting, plausible and attractive. *(This occurrence is related to the community operation: Empowerment.)* It is important to achieve one-set of goals before re-aligning to pursue the next set of goals!

"The four strategies to generate momentum are crucial for success. They have been extrapolated from successes in other cities and proven through multiple implementations of the Organic Environment. These strategies provide an execution plan to organically accelerate a city or region's economy."

~ Dr. Bernard Franklin

In Kansas City, StartKC had set each of these four strategies with its coordinator teams and government and civic leaders, and decided to focus on high-growth, technology, and general entrepreneurship as a whole. As an example, here is a summary *(slightly modified for confidentiality purposes and reduced for brevity)* of the four strategies that StartKC embraced.

Facilitated Strategies	Target Outcomes
Set Entrepreneur Goals	Attract 25 entrepreneurial startups in StartPath. 15 growing businesses in GrowPath.
Set Community Goals	The goals to be achieved by the coordinator teams, are: 5 coaches 10 mentors 10 investors 2 event sponsors
Facilitate Action Plan	Agree upon a 90-day plan that utilizes experiential events to incentivize and attract the coaches, mentors, investors, event sponsors, and entrepreneurs. The experiential event, startFEST+DEMO, is to be held at the conclusion of the 90-days to act as the impending event and to promote the successes achieved.

Milestone Periods	Set Milestones
30-Day	7 startups 3 growing businesses 1 coach 2 mentors 2 investors 3 event sponsor prospects
60-Day	20 startups 10 growing businesses 3 coaches 5 mentors 5 investors 1 event sponsor confirmed
90-Day	25 startups 15 growing businesses 5 coaches 10 mentors 10 investors 2 event sponsors confirmed

The Organic Entrepreneur Economy

As you can see, StartKC started out small, but allowing the community to organically foster that growth was the key. A more aggressive and expensive strategy for achieving early and strong results is often more appealing, but this approach is rarely embraced and supported by the community...and becomes an expected entitlement instead. This is best described in the wise tale: *"Give a man a fish, Feed him for a day. Teach him how to fish, And feed him for a lifetime."* The point is that as the Organic Environment gains community ownership and awareness, it will quickly accelerate to attract use by the entrepreneur masses. This was the case for StartKC, as can be seen by the entrepreneur environment in Kansas City today.

"Setting the community's expectations for what is possible from the Organic Environment and then exceeding the expectations will generate an incredible amount of momentum and support. Moreover, detailing how the goals were met and what the community can do to further exceed the expectations provides the masses an opportunity to put their excitement into action for the city or region's economy."

~ Barry J Crocker

Facilitating this guidepost is important to the success of the Organic Environment. The four strategies will not only guide the implementation of the Organic Environment and progress for entrepreneurs, but also the growth of the community, its culture, and the city's or region's economy. Government and civic leaders need to remember that it all starts with the first step: targeting the desired community outcomes for the city or region.

It is critical that these four strategies be heavily integrated, along with the implementation of the Organic Environment and Infrastructures, as this provides a refined perspective for the desired goals and how the coordinator team works to achieve them.

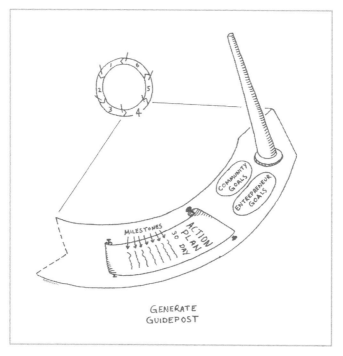

Generate Guidepost

Guidepost 5: Monitor

"There are two possible outcomes: if the result confirms the hypothesis, then you've made a measurement. If the result is contrary to the hypothesis, then you've made a discovery."
~ Enrico Fermi

"Our Organic Environment, GrowBlueSprings, operates almost completely through the community with the EDC operating principally as a "facilitator" to help with meeting venues, associated food & beverages, and resource guidance when needed. This innately empowers the community to act and engage with its entrepreneurs. A sense of empowerment coupled with metrics allows Blue Springs to focus its attention on helping troubled entrepreneurs, as well as supporting those in high-growth stages."

~ Brien M. Starner

Traditionally monitoring the progress of entrepreneurs as they start or grow businesses has been all but impossible, except when they are interacting within a specific incubator or entrepreneur program. The reason is that no one knows what specifically to track, how to monitor the progress, and what metrics predict future outcomes. The Organic Environment and infrastructures have provided the solution and even built the mechanisms to monitor and record useful metrics. Those mechanisms are the coordinator teams and the entrepreneur operations. In each community and entrepreneur operation there are analytics that are likely to be valuable to track...such as involvements, usage, and outcomes.

Every community, coordinator team, and government and civic leader should identify the metrics and information that they want to monitor based on their desired direction and outcomes. When there is still a knowledge gap between the desired outcome and what metric will help to predict that target, there are two options: 1) Ask the Coordinators for their Insights, and 2) Use Trial and Error. *(Trial and Error may seem a bit elementary, but remember you are getting ready to purposefully create and guide entrepreneurship...something you likely thought was impossible before beginning to read this book. So in this context, the Trial and Error Monitoring is directed towards learning what metrics help predict outcomes, previously considered impossible. Regardless of what is found, the insights will be a new discovery!)*

If you remember, in Kansas City StartKC decided to focus on high-growth, technology, and general entrepreneurship. Per this focus, here are the periodical results in this modified scenario were measured at each milestone.

Milestone Periods	Set Milestones	Achieved Milestones
30-Day	7 startups 3 growing businesses 1 coach 2 mentors 2 investors 3 event sponsor prospects	5 startups 3 growing businesses 2 coach 1 mentors 0 investors 1 event sponsor prospects
60-Day	20 startups 10 growing businesses 3 coaches 5 mentors 5 investors 1 event sponsor confirmed	18 startups 11 growing businesses 4 coaches 5 mentors 2 investors 2 event sponsors confirmed

90-Day	25 startups	35 startups
	15 growing businesses	15 growing businesses
	5 coaches	6 coaches
	10 mentors	15 mentors
	10 investors	15 investors
	2 event sponsors confirmed	3 event sponsors confirmed

Through community support of each operation, we were able to exceed these goals, track the results, and demonstrate the successes. Soon after we achieved these goals, the reporting and enrollment processes were automated to reduce the amount of time required from the coordinator teams and to report the metrics in near real-time. Thus the metrics helped us to realize that the strategies that we implemented for StartKC were effective and worth repeating in other Organic Environments.

"The results from StartKC, while abbreviated, demonstrate the effectiveness of the Organic Environment and infrastructures. This integrated "strategy" can and has accelerated the economy, the community, and entrepreneurship in multiple cities and regions. StartKC has provided the early proof for how to grow a community's economy through organic fostering of entrepreneurship."

~ Lisa Franklin

The advantage of monitoring metrics within the Organic Environment from the coordinator teams and the Infrastructures, is that all of the operations and metrics are interconnected. This allowed the insights to be more applicable and insightful across the entire entrepreneur and community environments. This is a clear advantage over having to independently monitor each operation, each program, or each person involved and then try to combine the data after the fact to find correlations. Monitoring metrics within the Organic Environment provide clarity within the data and an ease of collection. Consequently, government and civic leaders, the community, and coordinators have greater access to information that will help guide better decisions for the city's or region's economy.

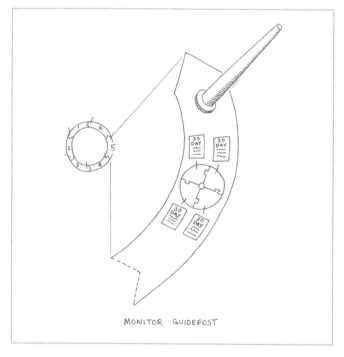

Monitor Guidepost

Guidepost 6: Empower! Empower! Empower!

"As we look ahead into the next century, leaders will be those who empower others." ~ Bill Gates

"To amplify success a community of individuals must be empowered. Grassroots efforts are largely mobilized by Doers, but the influencers that attract the communal masses to participate must also be recognized and given a seat at the table. Their influence can multiply the number of people involved and the outcomes that can be achieved."

~ Barry J Crocker

The Empowerment Guidepost is the biggy! It is the only guidepost that will actually move the community and entrepreneurs past the iconic tipping point and allow the Organic Environment to achieve critical mass. Empowering the community and entrepreneurs will lead to exponentially more developments and growth than the government or civic leaders could have ever planned or achieved. This is the point where the community and entrepreneurs become partners with the government and civic leadership in growing the economy!

For StartKC empowerment yielded social entrepreneurs who desired to build startup incubators and other creative mechanisms for supporting entrepreneurs. These social entrepreneurs were excited by the momentum and entrepreneur activity they perceived in their community and were motivated to help grow their city or region. One such example is Weston Bergmann, one of the cofounders of BetaBlox. Weston was excited about Kansas City's entrepreneur environment and was seeking a better way to help entrepreneurs accelerate their road to success. Since conception, BetaBlox has flourished by helping dozens of entrepreneurs start up and grow their businesses. Weston, along with his cofounders, have become incubator experts in the region, helping other incubators learn how to attract and better help entrepreneurs achieve success.

Growing the Organic Environment, while empowering these social entrepreneurs to build community-focused businesses, creates a ripple effect that will spread to exponentially grow entrepreneurship throughout the city or region. This *'Game Changer'* only manifests itself in a systematic method that supports entrepreneurs and the community, *The Organic Entrepreneur Economy*. If you look in Kansas City today there is a broad array of social and community focused businesses. Many were directly supported by StartKC, and many more simply sprouted when empowered by the growing economy they perceived in their community. Remember, the community and social entrepreneurs' empowerment is only sparked when entrepreneurial momentum is perceived in a city or region.

"This Game Changer IS the outcome that I, along with the other Advisory Experts, have been focused on for many years. There is now a solution to guide communities and their leaders on how to systematically grow entrepreneurship and their economy. This is a vision realized!"

~ Corey J. Mehaffy

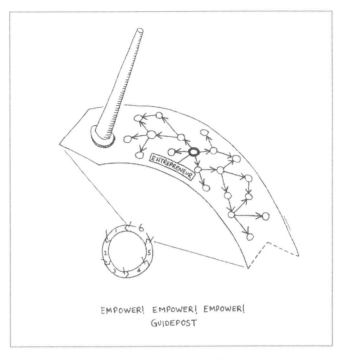

Empower! Empower! Empower! Guidepost

The Organic Environment Guideposts Review

Utilizing the guideposts offers government and civic leaders a more detailed framework to facilitate and empower the Community Audiences to foster entrepreneurship. The guideposts provide a "build schedule" of sorts to help government and civic leaders, as well as coordinator teams, effectively construct their branded Organic Environment in just 18 - 24 months. Doing so will organically yield a vibrant entrepreneurial community that will support a growing economy!

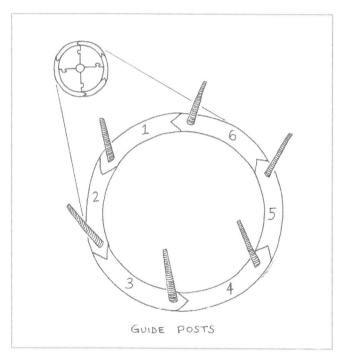

6 Guideposts

"The Organic Environment sets cities and regions up for creating a physical "Entrepreneur City," similar to an entertainment district, where entrepreneurs can go day or night to get the insights and support they need. Communities should look to build "Entrepreneur Cities" that attract and support entrepreneurial activities!"

~Jo Anne Gabbert

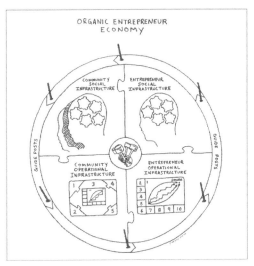

The complete *Organic Entrepreneur Economy*:
Organic Environment, four Infrastructures and 6 Guideposts

Chapter 10:

The Starting Line

Government and civic leaders who are seeking to exponentially grow their economy now have the operational tools and proven blueprints to understand and achieve their desired outcomes. Through the Organic Environment methodology, Infrastructures, and Guideposts, a city or region can now understand entrepreneurs and related community intricacies to foster the creation and growth of businesses. Throughout *The Organic Entrepreneur Economy,* that target outcome has been to achieve a critical mass of support from the community and from potential entrepreneurs who are embracing their ideas, and yet reaching this point is really just the beginning of the growth period, the **"starting line"** if you will. Reaching the starting line is as challenging as it is rare.

Lisa Franklin, Manager of

"The Organic Environment and Infrastructures are the new economic development blueprints for building community-led economies on an organically accelerated timetable. City and regional leaders will have greater tools to grow their economy, increase the job base, and foster a more supportive community and entrepreneurial environment."

~ Lisa Franklin

Economic Development and LocationOne at Kansas City Power & Light, has seen communities and their leaders utilize the Organic Environment and the Infrastructures to provide the necessary footing to foster and cultivate entrepreneurship in a city or region. Lisa's and KCP&L's support of multiple Organic Environments led them to witness a transformational change from the Infrastructures, which was often amplified by later initiatives. In Kansas City, StartKC's Organic Environment preceded Google Fiber, and, in essence, set the stage and prepped the economic engine at the starting line. Google Fiber's presence and initiatives super-charged the entrepreneurial community coming off the line. Growth after the critical mass "starting line" is when a community, its entrepreneurs, and the local economy really begin to accelerate.

> *"The reemergence of Kansas City's entrepreneur environment has come as a result of the community's support of entrepreneurship. Google Fiber has expanded the awareness and support of entrepreneurship to the local, regional and national communities. In my opinion, the creation of this entrepreneurial charge started before Google arrived, and was in part fueled early on by Kansas City's community-led Organic Environment - StartKC."*
>
> *~ Dr. Bernard Franklin*

The Organic Entrepreneur Economy really is a complete guide for cities or regions to achieve economic stability and growth through the power of entrepreneurship and their community. If you are still skeptical, listen to the perspectives of three additional government and civic leaders who have built and are facilitating community-branded Organic Environments.

Case Study: Grow Mid-Missouri

Corey Mehaffy – GrowMidMo.com – Moberly, Missouri – Grow Mid-Missouri serves a 16-County Rural Region of Northeast Missouri.

The Board and staff of the Moberly Area Economic Development Corporation (MAEDC) have long taken a three-pronged approach to economic development in the region… Business Retention & Expansion, Business Attraction and Entrepreneurship. In the past, MAEDC staff have collaborated with numerous partner organizations in an effort to piece together support for local entrepreneurs. With recent developments in the national economy over the last several years, we recognized a growing demand for rural entrepreneurial assistance. In effort to satisfy this need for our partner counties MAEDC collaborated with the Moberly Area Chamber of Commerce and the Moberly Area Community College to create a new organization dedicated to entrepreneurial development in our region. And so, Grow Mid-Missouri was created.

The Grow Mid-Missouri core team quickly recognized the need to establish an organic entrepreneurial ecosystem to support growth in our region. After learning statistics regarding failure rates in start-up businesses and cross-referencing those with the high success rates experienced by franchise business start-ups it became evident that the difference between the two groups was the "structure" that was available to assist business owners. It became evident that we needed to put an entrepreneurial infrastructure in place to provide relevant support to entrepreneurs in our region who wanted to start a new business or grow their existing business.

In a recent conversation with MAEDC Board Chair Russ Freed, we reflected on some of the tremendous examples of successful entrepreneurship we have in the MAEDC Region. One example is Orscheln Industries where in the 1930's with a complaint from one of the fleet drivers regarding parking brake issues, Al Orscheln sketched out a design (the first "overcenter" parking brake), built one in the shop, and installed it on a truck going to St. Louis. Another example is Mack Hils who in 1973 began building fasteners for antique truck beds in the basement of his home on the way to building Mack Hils, Inc. into the successful company it is today. Another example came in 1967 as Joe and Hildegarde Knaebel had a dream of owning their own business. It would be an uphill battle, with seven children, lots of bills, and very limited financial resources. Nonetheless, with the help of a few close friends, and a great banker, their business was started at the kitchen table of their home. From this humble beginning a very successful business know as Mid-Am Building Supply was built. Each of these unique businesses started with one idea and limited resources and are now some of the largest employers in Northeast Missouri.

Another example that came to mind during our conversation was the impact the leasing industry has had on Moberly and the surrounding area over the last 30 years. While the industry has certainly downsized in the area, today this sector is still responsible for some of the highest paying jobs in Randolph County. At one point just a few years ago, Moberly Missouri was known as the "rural" leasing capital of the world. Companies like GE Capital, Citi-Capital and Dolphin Capital, to name a few, had a presence in Moberly. Russ commented that even this important sector in the Moberly business community started with an entrepreneurial idea and investment. Barry

Orscheln, son of Don, started a commercial leasing company in the late 1970's, which became an industry leader prior to its sale to Chase Manhattan Bank in 1986. This one investment led other larger companies to make similar investments in the community and many of these companies maintain a presence in Moberly today. This continued support of entrepreneurship has allowed Moberly to become known as "the place to be" for entrepreneurs.

The Grow Mid-Missouri (GMM) core team has been very happy with the results we've seen over the first year of operating our Organic Environment. We've seen a number of community leaders engage in the program leading to a great deal of public interest. GMM has hosted a number of successful events including startFEST and PitchON events which led to a number of our entrepreneurs receiving funding for their projects from our investor network. In fact, several of Grow Mid-Missouri's entrepreneurs have been recognized by the Missouri Small Business Technology and Development Center entrepreneurship program receiving the prestigious "Rising Star" award.

The recent addition of the Grow Mid-Missouri Organic Environment had an immediate positive impact on our ability to serve entrepreneurs in the region and has spurred significant growth. The formation of our Organic Environment has allowed us to bring all the necessary resources to support entrepreneurial growth together in one program. Our team understood that most entrepreneurs are either working another job or at the very least have other commitments while at the same time trying to start their new venture. With that said, it was important for our team to make these resources available to our entrepreneurs when it was convenient for their schedules and not just when our team was available to assist. The addition of the online paths allows our entrepreneurs to work on projects on their schedule at their own pace. This component was critical to our program design and to its ultimate success.

One of our local entrepreneurs came to the Grow Mid-Missouri Organic Environment as a junior in high school. Becca Burkhart of Holdems, LLC has a number of very creative products she has designed and is taking to the market place. GMM allowed Becca to complete a viable business plan as well as financial projects. Becca ultimately competed in a local PitchON event and was introduced to the GMM investor network. With the financial assistance she received from the GMM investor network Becca has been able to take one of her products from design phase to full scale production, which in turn led to a national contract with a sporting goods distributor. As a side bonus Becca's products are being produced by a local manufacturing company.

Another of our Grow Mid-Missouri entrepreneurs came to the program all the way from Minnesota. An MAEDC staff member was attending a "pitch-type" event hosted by a group in Minnesota for companies that are looking to grow their business. Paul Koenig was one of the CEO's who presented at the event with a great idea and potential product. An invitation was extended to travel to the MAEDC Region which eventually led to Paul joining the GMM paths and presenting his company at one of our GMM events. Following Paul's visits to the region a relationship was established with one of the members of the GMM investor network and a new partnership called Azztec was formed. The company's initial pilot plant has been assembled in Monroe City, Missouri with new product development underway as well.

The Organic Environment is a proven method for entrepreneurial development and has been instrumental in our team's success. Armed with a rich heritage of entrepreneurship in Randolph County and the proven resources provided by the Grow Mid-Missouri Organic Environment our core team is excited for the future of entrepreneurship in our region.

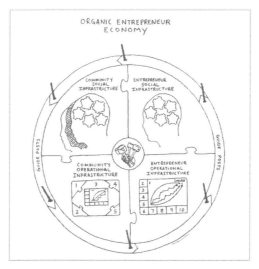

**Grow Mid-Missouri's Organic Entrepreneur
Economy Blueprint**

Case Study: BOOST Lee's Summit

Mark Dickey - BOOSTLeesSummit.com - Lee's Summit, Missouri - BOOST Lee's Summit serves the suburban community of Kansas City with a population of about 90,000 people.

As BOOST Lee's Summit approaches its first year of operation and nears critical mass, or the Starting Line, we are looking to up our game by adding new components to customize our Organic Environment. From our viewpoint, it is an organic progression towards growth requiring a greater combination of support mechanisms and tools to achieve. As we advance our offerings, not only to those desiring to start a business, but to existing businesses that desire growth, new infrastructures need to be developed – whether mentors, coaches, business resources or most importantly, processes. As client pipelines begin to mature, managing and accommodating client's needs requires additional resources and capabilities and improved, responsive and efficient systems.

To enhance momentum and accelerate client achievements, a physical presence is a logical advancement to program enhancement. Having a "sense of place", where the entrepreneurial community and clients can interact, connect and share provides for the enhancement of the experience and advances them quickly to their individual end goals. That is the next BIG step for BOOST Lee's Summit - establishing a physical footprint and enhancing its stature as the "first in the minds" of burgeoning entrepreneurs, existing businesses and those that interact and support them.

Having launched the Organic Environment and Infrastructures within the past year there has been little time to contemplate the various aspects of what it takes to create and sustain a viable and relevant effort. So, when asked to pen a few reflective paragraphs for *The Organic Entrepreneur Economy*, I jumped at the chance to finally step back and assess the key elements that are driving BOOST Lee's Summit's success.

To ensure brevity, I'll label the key elements as I perceive them to be the "Five C's:"

1. Commitment

2. Communication

3. Collaboration

4. Creativity

5. Can-do Attitude

Each of these is an essential rudiment for any endeavor, but especially when attempting something which is foreign to those stakeholders within your community that have always seen economic development from a very strict, conventional view.

When attempting to create a new culture by competing against entrenched thought processes, trust me when I say you better be committed to the task at hand. Persistence is vital as you will have the critics and the nay-sayers beating their drum loud and clear that this "new and very different" approach cannot possibly be effective. Or the oldest mantra on the planet, "We've never done it this way." At each step along the way, you will need to persevere the slings and arrows and stay positive, knowing that what you are doing is for the future of your community, whether they "get it" or not. I kept reminding myself of the bigger purpose of our efforts: to create wealth and develop the next generation leadership within our community.

I found that the more opportunities I had to explain what

we were attempting to do and how we were going about it, I gradually gained the acceptance of key community leaders. I quickly discovered that effectively articulating the vision and the approach we were taking to achieve that vision was key to breaking down the barriers of those that felt threatened by the unknown. Their fear, and therefore their lack of acceptance, was that of unfamiliarity or trepidation. By taking the time to explain the changing economic development playing field that we find ourselves engaged in and how we can have success with the creation of an established, system-based entrepreneurial ecosystem, we gained their confidence and their willingness to help. Even after nearly a year of operation and some significant successes under the belt, I find myself constantly reiterating the vision, reassuring people and providing opportunities for others who are just now hearing about BOOST Lee's Summit to plug-in.

Collaboration is gained through acceptance. Without the various sectors of the community pulling in one consistent direction, committed to a coherent and well-structured approach to establishing and operating an Organic Environment, the effort can languish and lose momentum. When beginning this venture, I observed that there existed fragmentation with those agencies and entities that were currently involved in economic development. By introducing a whole new concept and new approach, I was able to start at square one and create a collaborative process that wasn't tied to out-dated, bureaucratic processes and "turf" issues. The business community was the driving force behind the strong collaborative processes that exist today. They demanded a change, brought forth a new, solid approach and gained the acceptance of those that cater to businesses' needs.

One area that was definitely challenging, but recognized as

essential, was the creativity necessary to compliment and drive the development and operational aspects of the BOOST Lee's Summit Organic Environment. We quickly discovered that today's entrepreneurs converse differently, think differently, find their information differently and view a community's traditional infrastructure *(government, conventional lenders, economic developers, etc.)* very differently. Their interpretations are reality, so gaining their acceptance and participation requires creativity – a new speak. Employing creativity generates and encourages excitement, anticipation for something that has relevancy and exudes confidence that the venture *(BOOST Lee's Summit)* is sustainable and will result in positive, substantial outcomes. Attracting the new breed of entrepreneur, that next generation of leader to your community, necessitates new approaches, new means of communication and reaching out to nonconventional establishments and entrepreneurial communities. We have discovered that creatively positioning ourselves as an exciting, welcoming venture that holds the promise of success is critical to building activity within the community-led Organic Environment, which in turn, gets the knocks on the door, the telephones ringing and social media buzzing.

Lastly, and just as important as the first four "C's", possessing a Can-do Attitude. I should probably rephrase and say, a Can-do, Never Give-up Attitude. Throughout the development of the BOOST Lee's Summit program and the first couple months of operation, there were those weeks of just grinding – trying to gain footholds on so many levels. It was a fun, exhaustive experience, and one that is to be cherished. Establishing that "failure is not an option" mindset, for you know what the outcome can and will be, is the sustenance that injects the energy for the new economy that is being built and the cultural change that is necessary for future successes. All the best to you and your community as you begin your journey to create your unique Organic Environment.

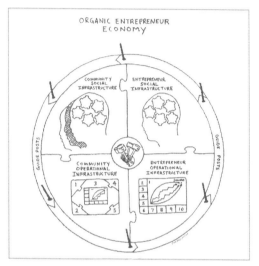

**BOOST Lee's Summit's Organic Entrepreneur
Economy Blueprint**

Case Study: Grow Blue Springs

Brien M. Starner - GrowBlueSprings.com - Blue Springs, Missouri - Grow Blue Springs serves a suburb of Kansas City with a community population of approximately 55,000.

The Blue Springs Economic Development Corporation (EDC) was introduced to StartKC's Organic Environment several years ago after one of our entrepreneurs had attended a GrowFEST. The entrepreneur reported back that the energy in the room was electric and the abnormally high concentration of angel investors, entrepreneurs, and corporate leaders were incredibly inviting and supportive. After receiving this report, the EDC researched StartKC and discovered that a small team of entrepreneurs were offering their fellow entrepreneurs a systematic process that increased their likelihood of success and created significant opportunities for their peers to gain access to capital, promotions, mentoring, coaching, and much more. Surprisingly this end-to-end entrepreneur ecosystem was being facilitated by only a handful of entrepreneurs; I was expecting to find dozens of staff members. When we learned that their key to operating the ecosystem was empowering the Kansas City community to play specific support roles without any direct compensation, I knew this was an approach I had to learn more about.

At the time StartKC, Kansas City's Organic Environment, was leading the entrepreneurial charge in the city by bringing together an "underground" network of technology entrepreneurs alongside more established government and corporate leaders. My counterpart at the Kansas City's Economic Development Corporation, Jeff Kaczmarek, had conveyed his excitement about the magnitude of entrepreneurs and community leaders that were working together due to StartKC.

In 2009 the Blue Springs EDC reached out to StartKC's entrepreneurs to learn if the Organic Environment could be replicated in Blue Springs. I was initially skeptical of the approach, because it relied heavily on community involvement and focused on hundreds of entrepreneurial businesses that were off our radar. During one session, I challenged the StartKC entrepreneurs to prove to me that the community would support this program and that there were growing entrepreneurial businesses in our community operating off the radar. No sooner had I made the challenge to this group than they used live social media to pinpoint and gain confirmation from a local entrepreneur in the event planning business, who also was facilitating a network of 30-something female entrepreneurs. The local entrepreneur expressed interest in being involved...during that same meeting. At this point, I knew the approach had merit.

Long story short, in 2010 we enthusiastically chose to implement the Organic Environment to begin supporting the entrepreneur masses in Blue Springs. The Organic Environment and infrastructures came with operational manuals that walked my EDC and business and civic leadership team through recruiting the community coordinators, training them, and then creating an action plan to populate the community's Organic Environment: GrowBlueSprings! Within six months GrowBlueSprings was operational in fostering entrepreneurship and gaining support from throughout the community in both known and unknown quarters. Soon after the launch, my team quickly realized the benefits the fully integrated ecosystem could bring to the community, and we were able to identify the organic acceleration happening throughout Blue Springs, Missouri.

Within nine months, GrowBlueSprings had two experiential events that attracted an audience of over 100 to support nine entrepreneurs. A pivotal highlight from the event was helping a local biotech company connect with investors, which resulted in a high, six-figure investment. The Organic Environment's structure and the Blue Springs' community had proven itself capable by attracting these growing businesses and angel investors to come together in our city to create positive growth! From there the community coordinators began to attract more entrepreneurs and participants, advocate for greater participation in entrepreneurship, and were even empowered enough to host additional experiential events. Perhaps the most important and significant take away, the Blue Springs EDC only had to support the Organic Environment, because the community coordinators took ownership and charge of the majority of the work to implement the action plan!

One example of the community coordinator's empowerment is the creation of the recent Retail PitchON! hosted by five cities in Jackson County, Missouri: Blue Springs, Lee's Summit, Independence, Oak Grove, and Grain Valley. GrowBlueSprings and BoostLeesSummit already had Organic Environment's in place, which significantly aided efforts to make this event successful in spotlighting the many retail businesses located in these communities. The experiential event also offered an opportunity for corporate sponsors to both buy and judge which retailers were the best by purchasing products as a way of voting. This event was attended by over 300 plus businesses and members of the public, and it had strong support from Jackson County's Economic Development program!

GrowBlueSprings has become and remains one of the EDC's

top program priorities, and the Organic Environment has a direct impact on growing jobs, fostering small business growth, and bolstering the economy and motivation among entrepreneurs to come forward and get involved. GrowBlueSprings has attracted a growing following and involvement from throughout the community, and that involvement is being utilized by the EDC to support other programs and initiatives. To compare where we started and where we are today, it is amazing how much our community has accomplished, learned and is taking ownership of in just a few short years. It is literally changing the community's economy, culture and improving its vision of where the community sees itself now and in the near future.

In addition, GrowBlueSprings strengthens our overall economic development strategy by fostering an environment that is more tolerant and supportive of small business, startup and entrepreneurial risks, needs and economic impact. This is now extending into the classrooms of our two local high schools, and as the seeds of our future are planted and nurtured with today's business opportunity, it is also attracting the voice, passion and interest of our talented youth! Grow Blue Springs and our Organic Entrepreneurial Environment will have the most lasting and transformative impacts for positive growth and change of any initiative that our EDC or community could ever undertake, and we're seeing these results now just a few years after "jumping in" with both feet. I invite you to learn more about how this initiative can change your community's economic future for the better by reading further, asking questions and taking action.

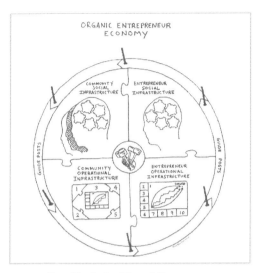

**Grow Blue Springs' Organic Entrepreneur
Economy Blueprint**

Conclusion

These case studies prove the validity of *The Organic Entrepreneur Economy*. This blueprint for fostering entrepreneurship and organically accelerating an economy can be achieved in 18-24 months rather than decades.

Now that a few have led the way, don't you think it is time to join in re-starting the global economy....starting with YOUR city or region? What are you waiting for?

To reach any of the Advisory Experts or the social entrepreneurs about this book or further insights email:

OrganicEnvironment@EvisThrive.com

Authors

Seth Meinzen

Seth Meinzen is a nine-time serial entrepreneur who has been committed to starting and growing profitable businesses in the last 10 years. During that time Seth gained valuable experiences from a few business failures, but also subsequent wins including taking a startup full-circle to a sale. In addition, Seth has been fortunate enough to have built more than a dozen support groups/networks, five successful events and conferences, and consulted hundreds of entrepreneurs and cities on how to start and grow businesses.

These experiences have lent Seth a first-hand understanding of the needs and resources required for startups and growing businesses to be successful. This led him to the inevitable question, "Is there a system or formula that can improve the chances of success for starting up and growing entrepreneurs' businesses, as well as the economies of their cities and regions?" This question has consumed Seth's energies for the last 7 years and with the support of the contributing authors has yielded an economy changing solution for cities and regions, as well as the entrepreneurs within them!

Growing up as a child with special needs, Seth's future seemed limited. However, his parents instilled in him a voracious work ethic and refused to allow him to accept these limitations. This drove Seth to finish high school, compete collegiately in crew and become the team captain, and graduate college with a Management and Marketing Degree (on the Dean's List) with an emphasis in Leadership Studies from Marietta College. Seth went straight from college into entrepreneurship and has achieved nearly impossible outcomes.

These life experiences have made Seth passionate about helping others, both personally and professionally. Seth's early experiences have taught him the power of collaboration and how to communicate complex topics and solutions. In addition, numerous magazines and websites have recognized Seth for his entrepreneurial results.

Seth is elated to be able to consult with cities, regions, and entrepreneurs on ways to grow their economies and for the challenge and opportunity to write The Organic Entrepreneur Economy with such a talented pool of collaborating authors! Most importantly, Seth is thankful to his Lord Jesus Christ for this opportunity to help others.

Steve Meinzen

Steve Meinzen has an undergraduate degree in Mechanical Engineering from the University of Kansas ('78) and an MBA from the University of Illinois ('97). Steve began his career In 1979 with John Deere with manufacturing engineering assignments at John Deere Tractor Assembly in Waterloo, IA. He subsequently held Field Service and Sales Management positions in several Midwestern states. Steve has also done project management work in South America large scale production agriculture and remote sensing applications. Steve served as Manager of Market and Customer Research at the John Deere Ag Marketing Center in Lenexa, KS.

He currently serves as an internal consultant on customer and market needs to the World Wide Tractor Platforms and Strategic Marketing Teams at Deere.

Co-Owner and co-Founder of Evis Consulting. Founded to provide community and economic development councils and Chambers of Commerce with a solution to rapidly foster entrepreneurship and a community culture that grows the local economy! Was instrumental in architecting the Organic Environment that accelerates the formation of naturally forming entrepreneur ecosystems.

Contributing Authors

Barry J. Crocker

Barry is a serial entre-preneur with a strong focus on technology. His first entrepreneurial venture was developing and launch-ing the first video-sharing platform designed for kids. KidsTube.com became one of the most trafficked user-generated video sites for kids. After it was sold, Barry began working with the EvisThrive team to develop educational products for businesses. Barry remains an advisor for KidsTube.com as well as handling all tech-related business for EvisThrive and overseeing the product development portion of the company.

Mark W. Dickey

Mark Dickey. IOM–
Currently the Vice Presi-
dent of the Lee's Summit
Chamber of Commerce,
his responsibilities include:
oversight of the Chamber's
Governmental Affairs pro-
gram, development and
delivery of business education and training programs,

oversight of strategic projects (including Boost Lee's Summit
, an entrepreneurial ecosystem) and community and economic
development activities. Mark has a strong background in community and economic development having spent over two
decades in municipal and state government operating community and economic development programs.

Mark also owned and operated a consulting firm in Des
Moines, Iowa, Comprehensive Housing Services, Inc., whose
focus was on developing affordable housing throughout the
state.

Mark is a graduate of Northwest Missouri State University,
with degrees in Public Administration and Business Administration.

Christopher Doroh

Chris is an entrepreneur as well as innovative and accomplished accounting professional with over seven years of accounting experience that includes four years as an accounting manager for a reputable title/ real estate company. As an accounting manager, Chris led the growth of an accounting department and expanded its size from a team of three accountants to twelve and the accounting responsibilities of one company to ten other sister companies. Chris has managed accounting for multiple organizations through the implementation of new accounting systems and aligning operations with finance resulting in cohesiveness within the organization.

Dr. Bernard Franklin

Dr. Bernard Franklin is a passionate urban community leader and a consultant to educational institutions, health and wellness organizations, organizations serving youth and families, and the civic community. Most recently, Dr. Franklin served as the President of Metropolitan Community College-Penn Valley in Kansas City. He is currently Assistant Vice President at Kansas State University and the President of Junior Achievement's Midwest Region.

A 1976 and 1996 graduate of Kansas State University, Dr. Franklin is considered one of the first African Americans to be elected student body president on a predominately Caucasian campus in the U.S. Dr. Franklin went on to make Kansas history books by becoming the youngest person ever appointed to the Kansas State Board of Regents at 24, and the youngest Chair of the Board at age 28. Dr. Franklin has been a Fellow for the Study of the United States Presidency, and has served on an advisory commission to the Carter Administration with Martin Luther King III and other prominent young African Americans.

Most recently, Dr. Franklin serve as Executive Director of Kauffman Scholars (2003-05), a $70 million, 20 year initiative funded by the Ewing Marion Kauffman Foundation to guide and support urban Kansas City 7th graders to high school graduation, and college graduation. Dr. Franklin has served as a member of the NFL Kansas City Chiefs professional counseling team. He was appointed by the Mayor of Kansas City, KS to co-chair the Mayors Task Force on Race and the Latin American Community, exploring ways the Latino and African American community could work together. Dr. Franklin has served on the board of Truman Medical Center, and the Community Advisory Board of the Federal Reserve Bank of KC. Finally, Dr. Franklin is a member of the Mayor's Bi-State Innovation Task Force, which has the charge of recommending how the Google Broadband fiber technology will be rolled out in the KC urban communities.

Dr. Franklin has twice been honored one of the 100 Most Influential African Americans in Kansas City (1998, 2009). The Greater Kansas City Chamber of Commerce honored him with their distinguished Leadership Award (2009) for contributions to urban education. The Kansas City Downtown Council awarded Franklin as an "Urban Hero" for his work in public education (2009).

Lisa Franklin

Lisa Franklin, CEcD, EDFP, is a recognized leader in the economic development profession. With more than 25 years of experience providing value to economic development organizations and communities as both a practitioner and consultant, she is frequently called upon to provide innovative solutions for economic development organizations to improve the overall effectiveness of technology-led initiatives.

As Manager of Economic Development for KCP&L, Lisa's primary responsibility is to administer and manage the LocationOne Information System (LOIS), an economic development site selection application that has grown rapidly over the last few years and now serves more than 8,000 communities across nearly 30 states. LocationOne has been recognized by numerous economic development organizations, including the International Economic Development Council and ESRI, as one of the leading economic development site selection applications in the marketplace. In 2012, Lisa's primary focus is launching one of the first nationwide iPhone and Android economic development site selection mobile applications and new LOIS Data Administration site for its users.

Prior to joining KCP&L, Lisa held positions with the Missouri Department of Economic Development, Jackson County Economic Development, Aquila and Real-Info, an economic development consulting company. Lisa is an active member of the International Economic Development Council (IEDC), the Council for Community and Economic Research (C2ER), Utility Economic Development Association (UEDA), the Missouri Economic Development (MEDC-Counselor) and the Blue Springs Economic Development Corporation (Board Member) where she resides.

Lisa received the designation "Certified Economic Developer" (CEcD) from IEDC in 1995 and her "Economic Development Financial Professional" (EDFP) certification in 1997. She holds a bachelor's degree in marketing and management from Missouri Southern State University in Joplin, Missouri.

Jo Anne Gabbert

Upon graduation from the University of Central Missouri, Jo Anne started her career in the telecommunications industry as an information technology analyst. After nine years with Southwestern Bell Telephone (now AT&T), Jo Anne joined Ernst and Young's Management Consulting group where she consulted in several different industries within publicly traded Fortune 500 Companies. Jo Anne specializes in management consulting and business advisory for companies of all sizes. Her expertise includes operational efficiency and effectiveness, strategic planning, customer service, project management, process and organizational design and development.

In 1999, Jo Anne founded management consulting company, Adams-Gabbert & Associates, Inc. Adams-Gabber specialized in operational excellence, project management, process improvement, change management, and strategic planning for a variety of industries.

In January 2008, Jo Anne sold Adams-Gabbert & Associates to the Bicknell Family Holding Company (BFHC) and in 2009 assumed the role of President of BFHC. In this role, Jo Anne instituted and chaired the advisory boards for 9 of the operating companies within the $400 million portfolio of companies. Jo Anne worked with the company presidents on strategic planning, leadership, management, operational excellence, cost containment, revenue growth and overall fiscal responsi-bility and accountability. In addition to overseeing the BFHC portfolio companies, Jo Anne performed CEO and COO roles, acquisition operational due diligence, and led the turnaround and/or shut down of company operations.

In June of 2011, Jo Anne resigned from the Bicknell Family Holding Company to start her latest company JAG Portfolio Services (JPS). JPS specializes in business advisory, executive coaching, large project management, acting CEO/COO and strategic planning.

Amongst her numerous company awards, Jo Anne has been personally recognized with the E&Y Entrepreneur of the Year Award in 2001, 2002 and 2004. In 2003, Jo Anne was recog-nized with the Women Who Mean Business Award. In 2009, Jo Anne was recognized as one of Midwest CEO Magazines Most Influential Women throughout Missouri, Kansas, Nebraska and Oklahoma and in 2010 Jo Anne was honored with the Legacy award for distinguished graduates from Longview Community College and as one of Kansas City's top female executives by Ingram's Magazine.

Over the last 12 years Jo Anne has served on numerous public and private boards and committees in the capacity of volunteer, director and/or advisory council. Jo Anne currently serves on the boards of The United Way of Greater Kansas City and The Boys and Girls Club of Greater Kansas City.

Matthew Hart

Matthew Hart is Vice President of Information Technology at Arise Virtual Solutions, the industry leader in providing onshore virtual customer service for fortune 500 companies. Matt came to Arise from Avaya, where he was the Senior Director of Technology Strategy and Development and ran a global development organization focused on remote product support and servicing technologies. Prior to Avaya, Matt spent a decade at Oracle Corporation, where he made his name as a database backup and recovery expert. Matt is the co-author of six technology books on Oracle software, he wrote the fiction series The Last Iteration, and is the author of the management and leadership book Middlework: Unlock the Underestimated and Unappreciated Secret to Success. Matt was born and raised in Idaho Falls, Idaho, before completing his education in Colorado Springs and settling down in Kansas City with his wife and two children.

Jeff Kaczmarek

Jeff Kaczmarek has more than thirty years of professional experience in economic development and is currently the Executive Director of the Prince William County Department of Economic Development.

Prior to joining Prince William County in April 2012, Mr. Kaczmarek was the President and Chief Executive Officer of the Economic Development Corporation of Kansas City, Missouri, where he led a staff of over 30, with a budget exceeding $4 million in a board-directed 501 c) (4) organization serving as the City's economic development agency. From 2007, through mid-2011, the EDC was significantly involved in over 100 business projects which resulted in $1.6 billion in private sector investment and the creation or retention of over 11,000 jobs. The EDC also provided substantial assistance to over 30 development/redevelopment projects resulting in more than $2 billion in private investment.

During the period from 1999-2005, Mr. Kaczmarek served as Senior Vice President, Business Services and Community Development for the Michigan Economic Development Corporation, where he led MEDC's local community technical assistance, infrastructure financing, small business assistance, economic development job training and export promotion programs. MEDC was an award-winning, quasi-public development agency. Prior to his position with the MEDC, Mr. Kaczmarek served as the Director of Community and Economic Development for Oakland County Michigan, where he directed the operations of the Economic Development, Employment and Training and Community Development Divisions of this large metropolitan County near Detroit.

Mr. Kaczmarek earned a B.S. in Urban Planning from Michigan State University, did graduate work at Wayne State University and serves on various economic development organizations.

Danny Lobina

Danny Lobina is a skilled business advisor with over 15 years of business experience. Danny holds a Bachelor of Science in Economics and Finance, a Bachelor of Science in Management, and a Master of Business Administration. He specializes in consulting with small to medium sized businesses in the start-up and growth phases. He also works with businesses that have reached the maturity and decline phases to develop process improvement and turn-around strategies. Danny has taken a special interest in Economic Development and works closely with local organizations to improve the financial impact and job creation of Northeast and Central Missouri. Danny currently works as the Regional Director for the Missouri Small Business and Technology Development Center at Moberly Area Community College, overseeing a 16 county region with 2 offices including Moberly and Kirksville.

Professional development is a top priority, earning certifications as a Professional Business Coach, Economic Development Finance Professional, Economic Gardening Professional, Geographic Information Systems Specialist, and Certified Profit-Cents Advisor.

Danny is active in the community and is the Vice-President of the Moberly Area Chamber of Commerce, Board Member of the Missouri Rural Enterprise and Innovation Center,

Board Member of the Randolph Area YMCA, a member of the Strategic Planning Committee for the University of Missouri Business Development Program, the Moberly Area Community College Marketing Committee, and represents Randolph County on the Mark Twain Regional Council of Governments Transportation Committee.

Corey J. Mehaffy

Corey J. Mehaffy joined the staff of Moberly Area Economic Development Corporation as the President of the organization in February of 2008. As President, Mehaffy is responsible for all economic development efforts including business retention & expansion, business attraction and entrepreneurship in a four county region in North Central Missouri. In 2012 Mehaffy, along with two other partners founded Grow Mid-Missouri an entrepreneurial development program which serves 17 counties in northeast Missouri.

Prior to joining MAEDC Mehaffy served for five years as the Chief Operating Officer of Central Christian College of the Bible and one year as the COO of L&J Development, Inc. both of Moberly. Mehaffy came to CCCB after serving as the VP of Operations for Pike Mechanical, Inc. and serving as the Director of Operations and Business Development for Arona Corporation both of Des Moines Iowa. Mehaffy has held several senior management positions in a variety of industries.

Mehaffy serves as a Board Member of several civic and charitable organizations including the Moberly Regional Medical Center, Moberly Rotary Club, City of Moberly Tourism Advisory Council, Northeast Missouri Workforce Investment Board, Katharos Ministries, Northeast Evangelism, and the Randolph Area YMCA where he was recognized as the 2008

Board Volunteer of the Year. Mehaffy is a member of the Mid-west US-China Association (MWCA) as well as the American Chamber of Commerce China (AMCHAM).

Michie P. Slaughter

During his career as Vice President and member of the board of Marion Laboratories, Michie was a key influence in helping the founder and chairman, Ewing M. Kauffman, institutionalize his basic business philosophies. He was one of the primary architects of the leadership, organization and management development strategies employed by Marion during its dramatic growth from $50 million to $1.0 Billion in sales.

Michie helped found the Kauffman Center for Entrepreneurial Leadership at the Ewing Marion Kauffman in 1992 and served as its first Chairman and President. He was one of the designers of the Kauffman Fellows Program and served as a member of the board of the Center for Venture Education which educates and places Kauffman Fellows in leading US and International venture capital firms. He was named to the Board of the Ewing Marion Kauffman Foundation in 1998.

A graduate of Davidson College, he lead start-up and rapid growth projects at Abbott Laboratories and American Home Products Corporation before joining Marion. He has served as board member/advisor to a number of entrepreneurial ventures throughout the country and abroad. He served as member of the Babson College Entrepreneurial Advisory Board, the International Entrepreneur of the Year Institute Board, and the Board of the Helzberg Entrepreneur Mentoring Program. He is currently a Partner in 5th Dimension Strategies LLC, a consulting firm that helps clients build high performance organizations.

Brien M. Starner, CEcD

Brien M. Starner has been involved in professional economic development in public, corporate and public/private organizations for over 27 years, and is currently President of Blue Springs Economic Development Corporation (EDC) where he has worked since April 2005.

Brien has a BA in Public Administration and Political Science from William Jewell College, and is a Certified Economic Developer (CEcD), a professional designation through the International Economic Development Council. Brien has also completed professional coursework through the Institute for Organization Management operated by the US Chamber of Commerce.

Brien is the President of Blue Springs Economic Development Corporation, a non-profit economic development corporation with public and private investors whose mission is fostering business development, investment and job growth for Blue Springs, Missouri. Through Brien's efforts the corporation has more than 65 investing member partners, including a contract for services with the City, and investors that include the Chamber of Commerce, School District and Central Jackson County Fire Protection District. Among Brien's major work initiatives within the EDC are an entrepreneurial initiative known as

Grow Blue Springs; Blue Springs Industry Council; Missouri Innovation Park, INC and the development of the Missouri Innovation Park.

Brien has previously worked with Overland Park Economic Development Council in Overland Park, KS as the Director Economic Development, with Aquila, a power company with territories in Kansas City, Missouri, and Michigan as the Director Economic Development and Corporate Real Estate, with Leavenworth Area Development in Leavenworth, KS as their Executive Director, with Kansas City Area Development Council in Kansas City, MO as the Development Director, and with Green Hills Regional Planning Commission in Trenton, MO as the Community Planner.

9776690R00175

Made in the USA
San Bernardino, CA
27 March 2014